Sophocles: Ajax

D1596864

BRISTOL CLASSICAL PRESS COMPANIONS
TO GREEK AND ROMAN TRAGEDY

Series editor: Thomas Harrison

Also available

Euripides: Hippolytus
Sophie Mills

Euripides: Medea
William Allan

Seneca: Phaedra
Roland Mayer

Seneca: Thyestes
P.J. Davis

BRISTOL CLASSICAL PRESS COMPANIONS
TO GREEK AND ROMAN TRAGEDY

Sophocles: Ajax

Jon Hesk

Bristol Classical Press

Published by Bristol Classical Press 2012

Bristol Classical Press, an imprint of Bloomsbury Publishing Plc

Bloomsbury Publishing Plc
50 Bedford Square
London WC1B 3DP
www.bloomsburyacademic.com

Copyright © Jon Hesk 2003

First published by Gerald Duckworth & Co. Ltd. 2003

The author has asserted his rights under the Copyright, Designs and
Patents Act 1988 to be identified as the author of this work.

ISBN: 978 0 715 63047 1

A CIP catalogue record for this book is available from the British Library

Contents

Preface

I would like to thank the following individuals, groups and institutions for valuable assistance with this book and useful conversations about the *Ajax*: Deborah Blake (at Duckworth), Richard Buxton, Paul Cartledge, Pat Easterling, the Classics and Philosophy Departments at Wooster College, Ohio, Simon Goldhill, the Greek and Latin Department seminar at Ohio State University, Emily Greenwood, Stephen Halliwell, Glenis and John Hesk, Tom Harrison (a fine series editor), Katherine Hawley, Jim McGlew, Menno Pot (of the USA *Ajax FC* supporters club), Roger Rees, David Rosenbloom, the School of Classics seminar in St Andrews, Michael Silk, Victoria Wohl, Amanda Wrigley (of the *Archive of Greek and Roman Performances of Drama* in Oxford). I must acknowledge and thank Oxbow Books for kind permission to quote throughout from the prose translation of A. Garvie, *Sophocles: Ajax* (Warminster: Aris and Phillips, 1998). I also acknowledge and thank Cambridge University Press for kind permission to cite the verse translation of S. Dutta, *Sophocles: Ajax*, Cambridge Translations from Greek Drama (Cambridge: Cambridge University Press, 2001) on p. 115. The book is dedicated to the many students in Cambridge, Reading and St Andrews who have helped me to think about this challenging and fantastic play.

1

Playwright, Plot and Performance

Sophocles and *Ajax*

Sophocles lived a long and creatively productive life (*c.* 496-406/5 BC). His first victory in the tragic contest at the Athenian festival known as the City Dionysia was in 468 BC, when he beat no less an opponent than Aeschylus. The *Ajax* is one of Sophocles' five surviving tragedies for which we do not have anything like a secure date of performance. (Of the other two extant and complete plays, we know that *Philoctetes* was performed in 409 and that *Oedipus at Colonus* was staged posthumously in 401.) Sophocles seems to have written more than 120 plays (tragedies and satyr dramas) and to have had at least eighteen victories at the City Dionysia. We have fragments and/or titles for many of these. *Ajax* may not be Sophocles' most celebrated tragedy – *Antigone* and *Oedipus Tyrannus* surely compete for that accolade. But there is something uniquely dark and disturbing about its depiction of humiliation, madness, suicide and isolation. And there is something distinctively moving and paradoxically beautiful about the poetry, imagery and brutal rhetoric which the *Ajax's* characters use.

I have written this book in such a way that the reader is taken through every scene of *Ajax* sequentially. But the subsequent chapters are frequently punctuated by more general discussions which require knowledge of the whole play, so it will be helpful to give a brief outline of plot, structure and significant action immediately. The following division of the play into its constituent parts (episodes, odes etc.) does violence to the play's actual flow, richness and power, but it is important to realise that this tragedy, like all others, is shaped by certain conventions and traditional patterns.

Opening scene (prologue): 1-133. Like all tragic prologues, this scene provides the audience with all the information it needs to establish clearly what has happened and what is at issue. We are in Ajax's encampment during the Trojan war. It gradually emerges that Ajax has been angered by the Greeks' vote to award the arms of the fallen hero Achilles to Odysseus (the so-called 'Judgement of Arms'). The audience would know the tradition that Ajax and Odysseus had both been involved in the recovery of Achilles' body during combat but that the former hero had lost the Judgement. Ajax has now attempted to kill Agamemnon (leader of the Greek army) and his brother Menelaus (known together as the Atreids, meaning 'sons of Atreus'). But the goddess Athena has foiled Ajax's attack by visiting him with a delusional form of madness. This delusion has led him to slaughter the army's cattle, sheep and their herdsmen instead of the Atreids. The prologue begins with Odysseus searching for Ajax's whereabouts. Athena speaks to confirm what Ajax has done and reveals her part in it. She then summons Ajax from his tent – he is still gripped by madness and cannot see Odysseus. Odysseus feels pity for Ajax. Ajax retires to his tent and after a discussion of the vulnerability of mortals, Odysseus and Athena exit.

Choral entrance song (*parodos*): 134-200. A chorus of sailors under Ajax's command enter. They are worried by, and speculate upon, the rumours of Ajax's night-time raid. They cannot believe the rumours and hope that Ajax will defend his reputation.

First scene (first episode): 201-595. Ajax's concubine, Tecmessa, enters from his tent. She tells the sailors that the rumours are true. Ajax then enters – he appears to be sane but he expresses his hostility to the Atreids and Odysseus. He also speaks of his despair and shame at the slaughter of the livestock. In response to Ajax's claim that suicide is the only noble course of action, Tecmessa pleads with him to consider her and his family. Ajax demands to see his son Eurysaces and addresses him directly. Intransigent in the face of Tecmessa's pleading, he enters the tent. Tecmessa and Eurysaces also withdraw.

First choral ode (first *stasimon*): 596-645. In lyric metres characteristic of the *stasimon*, the Chorus sing of their homeland, Salamis. They describe the difficult conditions at Troy and their despair over Ajax's situation.

Second episode: 646-92. Ajax re-enters to deliver his so-called 'deception speech'. He seems to indicate a change of heart. He will purify himself in response to his crime and will yield to the gods and show reverence to the Atreids. Tecmessa and the Chorus are listening to his words and, having reassured them that all will be well, he exits alone.

Second *stasimon*: 694-718. The Chorus sing of their joy at Ajax's apparent change of heart.

Third episode: 719-865. A messenger arrives from the Greek camp to announce that Ajax's half-brother, Teucer, has returned to a hostile reception on account of Ajax's actions. He then tells of the prophet Calchas' warning that Ajax must not leave his tent if he is to remain alive. Athena is angry with Ajax for having acted impiously in the past – it seems that she will endanger him for this day only. Tecmessa enters to hear this news and organises a search for Ajax. The Chorus and Tecmessa exit.

There is now an imagined scene-change to a secluded grove near the seashore; some critics think that this constitutes a new episode. Ajax appears and makes his 'death speech'. Having invoked goddesses of vengeance (the Erinyes or 'Furies'), he curses the Atreids. He leaps on the sword which he has planted in the ground. This sword (which Hector gifted him after a duel) is the same weapon as that used in his raid on the livestock.

Fourth episode: 866-1184. This scene begins with the second entrance of the Chorus. Their exchanges among themselves and with Tecmessa constitute what ancient commentators called an *epiparodos*. The Chorus cannot find Ajax, but then a cry of despair indicates that Tecmessa has found his body. She sings a lament for him which expresses defiance towards his enemies. Teucer arrives, laments over Ajax's corpse and anticipates that his father Telamon will blame him. He is ready to bury Ajax's body. Menelaus enters and declares that the body must remain unburied. Teucer and Menelaus quarrel. Their argument is in

11

the common tragic format of the *agôn* ('contest' or 'debate scene'). Menelaus threatens violence and then exits. Teucer also exits to make ready a tomb for Ajax. Tecmessa and Eurysaces arrive to keep vigil by Ajax's body.

Third *stasimon* (1185-1222). The Chorus describe their life as combatants and imagine the peacetime pleasures they are missing. They long to be back in Salamis.

Final scene (*exodos*): 1223-1420. Teucer re-enters because he sees Agamemnon approaching the body. Teucer and Agamemnon engage in another *agôn*. Their quarrelling is then interrupted by Odysseus. Odysseus manages to persuade Agamemnon to allow Ajax's body to be buried. But Agamemnon will have no part in the funeral and he exits. Teucer acknowledges with surprise that Odysseus has acted as a good man but limits his role in the burial. Odysseus exits. The tragedy ends with the Chorus, Teucer and Eurysaces performing Ajax's burial rites. It is not clear whether Tecmessa is still a silent presence. The Chorus follow Teucer's praise of Ajax with the reflection that mortals can understand many things once they have seen them but that nobody knows how he will fare in the future.

What made Sophocles choose to present this story? We often like to look at the lives of writers for clues as to what inspired or guided their literary output. But it is very hard to disentangle truth from falsehood in the biographies and anecdotes about the three great Attic tragedians which proliferated from the third century BC onwards.[1] And 'biographical' approaches to tragedy are singularly unhelpful given the conventional nature of the genre, its mythical content and its festival context. Nevertheless, the following aspects of Sophocles' life and career are still significant for understanding our play.

First and foremost, it is important to realise that Sophocles was more successful than Aeschylus or Euripides in terms of his competitive record at the Dionysia. His surviving output and the biographical tradition both indicate that Sophocles was concerned to make the most of the theatrical possibilities and resources which were available to him and it was perhaps this willingness to experiment which made his tragedies so popular. We will see that *Ajax* makes good and perhaps pioneering use of spectacle and surprise, although one has to be sceptical of later biographical assertions about various theatrical innovations attributed to him. For example, we cannot be sure that he really did increase the size of the Chorus or invent the white boots which actors wore (*Life of Sophocles* 4-6). But these stories corroborate the sense we get from his surviving tragedies that Sophocles was immersed in the process of translating his texts into live theatre. One critic rightly remarks that 'much of Sophoclean theatricality resides in his dramatic use of significant objects and significant actions, especially entrances and exits'.[2] And there is some evidence to suggest that Sophocles frequently wrote with the vocal (and singing) strengths of particular actors in mind.[3] In our play, Ajax sings several lyric passages – these may have been tailored for a specific actor.

Sophocles' status as a prominent figure in democratic Athens did not wholly derive from his theatrical successes. In his fifties, he was a Treasurer of Athena and was one of the elected generals (*stratêgoi*) who served alongside Pericles. He may have held this office during the revolt of Samos in 441 BC (*FGrH* 324 Androtion F 38). This means that he was for a while as important as a cabinet minister in the United Kingdom. When the Athenian expedition to Sicily failed in 413 BC he was one of ten appointed advisers who dealt with the ensuing state of emergency (Aristotle *Rhetoric* 1419a25). These prominent political roles which Sophocles held during Athens' protracted and costly hostilities with Sparta are important background for our reading of *Ajax*. We will see that our tragedy speaks directly to the politics and effects of war, the limits of loyalty, and the competing claims of personal honour, family-ties and collective discipline.

Sophocles also played a significant religious role during and after his lifetime. He seems to have been a priest in the cult of the hero Halon. He was even involved in the establishment of a new cult of the healing god Asclepius. After his death, Sophocles was himself given the honours of a cult-hero under the new name of Dexion. I will discuss the nature and importance of hero-cult in Chapter 2, and we will see that Ajax's status as an object of such worship is of fundamental importance to our understanding of Sophocles' tragedy. The evidence for his life points to 'a special connection believed to exist between Sophocles and the heroes in the religious life of the city'.[4]

Ancient assessments of Sophocles' character and the style of his tragedy have often led modern critics to view his dramatic output as representing a middle ground between Aeschylus' grandiosity and Euripides' so-called 'realism' and smoothness. For example, Sophocles is supposed to have said he portrayed men 'as they ought to be' in contrast to Euripides who portrayed them 'as they are' (Aristotle *Poetics* 1460b33). Plutarch claims that Sophocles regarded his output as going through three phases, the first being the inflated style of Aeschylus, the second being crude and artificial and the third being the phase he thought was most suited to character portrayal and 'the best' (*Moralia* 79b). And there is a famous statement of the third-century philosopher Polemon that Sophocles was 'the tragic Homer' (*TGrF* IV T 115). These views have their merits in recognising that *Ajax* has an intimate relationship with Homeric epic and that its disturbing characterisations and varied tones partake of (and yet transcend) Aeschylean and Euripidean tendencies. But, as I will show, these pithy generalisations hardly do justice to Sophocles' distinctive exploration of moral complexity, poetic language and tragic action.

Dating and performance context

Although we do not have any external evidence for the date of the *Ajax*'s performance, scholars have often thought it to be one of the earliest of Sophocles' extant tragedies and some put it as early as 460 BC.[5] But there have also been cases made for the 450s, 440s and 430s. It would be nice to believe that Agamemnon's attack on Teucer's 'illegitimate' birth and Teucer's blistering reply are informed by Pericles' citizenship law of 451/0.[6] But even if this were certain (which it is not), we would still not be able to tie it to a particular decade in the second half of the fifth century, let alone a year.[7] Having said this, most scholars conjecture that the tragedy was written and performed some time in the 440s.

(188, 226). Ironically, the rumour *is* factually correct – although the Chorus's choice of words points to the incredible nature of the slaughter and (as *we* know) its divine inspiration. Because of its mythical qualities, then, Athenian audiences did not necessarily view a play like *Ajax* as a faithful depiction of real past events. But it would be over-simple to say that they therefore regarded the tragedy as 'untrue'. The fourth-century philosopher Aristotle makes the following observation:

> The writings of Herodotus could be put into verse and yet would still be a kind of history, whether written in metre or not. The real difference is this, that one tells what happened and the other what might happen. For this reason poetry is something more philosophical and serious than history, because poetry tends to give general truths while history gives particular facts.
>
> Aristotle *Poetics* 1451b1-7

Aristotle was prepared to see tragedy as truthful and yet not 'factual' by referring to a peculiar facility which fiction possesses, namely the creation of a possible world. The *Ajax* stages 'what might happen' and yet it offers its audience a particularly complex picture of the causes and reasons for such events. This is a possible world in which Ajax's suicide can be attributed to a wide range of (often incompatible or entangled) plot-features, characterisations and textual effects: divine anger, failures of reciprocity and justice, misunderstanding, calculated deception, madness, moments of lucidity, stubbornness, noblesse oblige, cultic destiny, and so on. The *Ajax* does indeed give us the 'general truth' that tragic events never have simple or single causes or explanations.

But if the *Ajax's* mythic quality yields transhistorical 'truths' about the complexities of responsibility, justice and causation, that does not make it *ahistorical*. Tragedy was not divorced from, or autonomous in relation to, the real world of its audience. The surviving tragedies of Aeschylus illustrate this point perfectly. The *Oresteia* dramatises a potent myth of vengeance but climaxes in Athens with the establishment of a homicide court (the Areopagus) which was a very real and controversial institution at the time of the first performance.[10] And the *Persians* is our one complete and extant example of a 'historical' tragedy where a real event (the defeat of the Persian forces by the Greeks at Salamis) is dramatised – it is particularly flattering to Athenian democracy.[11]

Sophocles' *Ajax* is not 'historical' like the *Persians*. Nor does it invoke an Athenian institution as explicitly as the *Oresteia*. But we will see that it does allude to a very concrete form of Athenian ritual. And while Ajax may not be an historical personage like Aeschylus' Xerxes, Shakespeare's Henry V or Spielberg's Oskar Schindler, it is important to remember that real and eminent Athenians such as Miltiades, Cimon and Alcibiades proudly claimed to be descended from him. Thus Ajax had a direct link with elite aristocrats who represented, led and sometimes cheated the Athenian *dêmos*. It may well be that Sophocles' Ajax was meant to capture the mixture of brilliance, arrogance and vulnerability which made the democracy's elite generals and advisers so politically ambiguous and ideologically problematic. But it is hard to read Ajax as an allegorical representation of a specific Athenian leader – not least because the game of finding a real personage behind our tragic hero yields a number of candidates who fit Ajax's profile in *some* respects but not in all.[12] For example, the heroic architect of victory at Salamis, Themistocles, was worshipped as a cult-hero despite his fall from grace and an initial refusal to bury him. But it is also possible to read Ajax as Cimon (Themistocles' arch-rival), and to show that *Odysseus* is the Themistoclean character. To see him as a much vaguer symbol of the propertied aristocrats who had dominated Athenian politics until the reforms of Ephialtes in 462 BC is more attractive but no less controversial or hard to prove.[13]

Ajax's main role in the 'real lives' of Athenians was as one of the major 'eponymous' Athenian heroes who each gave their names to the ten 'tribes' created by Cleisthenes in 508 BC. This meant that his statue stood in the Athenian Agora, watching over Athenian citizens as they went about their daily business (Pausanias 1.35.3). And a citizen watching the *Ajax* could have

20

epics.[19] Six of its eight *dramatis personae* are significant characters in the *Iliad* and *Odyssey*: Athena, Odysseus, Ajax, Teucer, Menelaus and Agamemnon. Furthermore, the *Odyssey* contains the earliest reference to the particular events with which Sophocles is concerned in the *Ajax*. When Odysseus goes down to the Underworld he encounters a number of heroes who died at Troy, including Ajax himself. This is how he describes the encounter:

> Now the rest of the souls of the perished dead stood
>   near me
> grieving, and each one spoke to me and told me of his
>   sorrows.
> Only the soul of Telamonian Ajax stood off
> at a distance from me, angry still over that decision
> I won against him, when beside the ships we disputed
> our cases for the arms of Achilles. His queenly mother
> set them as a prize, and the sons of the Trojans, with
>   Pallas Athene,
> judged; and I wish I had never won a contest like this,
> so high a head has gone under ground for the sake of
>   that armour.
>
> Homer *Odyssey* 11.541-9

Odysseus goes on to say that Ajax surpassed all the other Greeks in 'appearance' and 'actions': he was second only to Achilles (550-1). He then tries to talk to the ghost of Ajax, begging him to forget his anger against Odysseus over the affair of the 'cursed armour' (555). He describes Ajax as a 'tower' (*purgos*) who was sorely missed by the Greeks and whose death they grieved for as incessantly as Achilles' (556-7). Odysseus blames Zeus' hatred of the Greeks for Ajax's destruction but Ajax does not respond to these overtures. Odysseus is left telling his Phaeacian audience that 'despite his anger, he might have spoken, or I might have spoken to him' but instead, he went to seek the souls of other dead men (565-7).

This Homeric encounter shows that Sophocles' *Ajax* is partly dependent on certain elements derived from epic tradition. The

Judgement of Arms was a feature of Ajax's story which probably predated the writing down of the *Odyssey* in the eighth
century BC.[20] As Garvie puts it, '[T]he story is told so allusively
that one must suppose that it was already familiar to Homer's
audience.'[21] Odysseus does not tell us how Ajax died but he
clearly links his death to the Judgement and its outcome.
Certainly there are meagre fragments and summaries of other
epics from the post-Homeric Epic Cycle which indicate that
Ajax committed suicide and that Sophocles' plot adopts many
other elements of Ajax's downfall from eighth- to sixth-century
hexameter epic.[22] From Proclus' summary (fifth century AD),
we know that the epic *Aethiopis* (probably seventh century BC)
narrated Ajax's removal of Achilles' corpse from the battle
while Odysseus fought off the Trojans (L 507-9; D 47).
According to Proclus this epic ended with a dispute between the
two heroes over Achilles' armour. It may be that the *Aethiopis*
also told of how Agamemnon decided to devolve the 'judgement'
to some Trojan prisoners by asking them which of the two
heroes gave them more trouble. They replied that Odysseus was
more troublesome than Ajax and so the former was awarded the
arms of Achilles.

Either the *Aethiopis* or another lost epic called the *Little
Iliad* narrated Ajax's suicide at dawn (L 509; D 48). The *Little
Iliad* began with the judgement which, according to one fragment, was conducted by Greeks eavesdropping on two Trojan
girls arguing over Odysseus' and Ajax's qualities as warriors,
with the pro-Odysseus girl winning the debate 'by the forethought of Athena' (L 513; D 53-4). As with Sophocles' play,
then, this version puts Athena on Odysseus' side. It is possible
that the poem depicted this goddess hastening Ajax's destruction, but there is no evidence to support this. Proclus' summary
also tells us that the *Little Iliad* narrated Ajax's madness, his
attack on the booty and his subsequent suicide. The poem also
contained Agamemnon's angry refusal to cremate Ajax's
corpse: the body was buried in a coffin instead (L 513; D 54). So,
the following are all traditional epic episodes or themes which
Sophocles is drawing on in our play: (1) Odysseus and Ajax's
roles in the rescue of Achilles; (2) the dispute between them

does not simply stage Homeric material or dramatise an Homeric 'world view'. We have already seen that the *parodos* of *Ajax* contains some very specific and thematically significant reworkings of Homeric poetry which stress a dissonance between the tragic Ajax and his Iliadic self. Most famously and obviously, the scene in which Tecmessa pleads with Ajax not to commit suicide is an adoption and adaptation of the intimate scene in Homer's *Iliad* in which the Trojan hero Hector speaks with his wife and child (*Iliad* 6.369-481). But we will see that the ways in which this scene diverges from its Homeric 'model' underline the specificity and distinctiveness of Ajax's and Tecmessa's characters and situations.[32]

The idea that a tragedy would provoke an audience to recall, compare and mentally cross-reference episodes and language from Homeric epic is not far-fetched. All the evidence points to Homer being performed, recited and read regularly in fifth-century Athens: a major public festival, the Panathenaia, included contests where professional singers (rhapsodes) and lyre-players performed sections of Homer to a citizen audience. Niceratus, one of Socrates' rich interlocutors in Xenophon's *Symposium*, claims that he knows the *Iliad* and *Odyssey* by heart and that he hears recitations from them every day (Xenophon *Symposium* 3.5-9).[33] Socrates responds by attributing unrivalled stupidity to the 'tribe of rhapsodes', but it is noteworthy that Niceratus is citing his knowledge of Homer as an example of wisdom (*sophia*) and beneficial knowledge. Furthermore, Niceratus was made to learn all of Homer because, he says, his father was 'anxious to see me develop into a good man (*anêr agathos*)'. This Greek phrase does not just mean 'morally good man': in the markedly democratic speeches proclaimed at Athens' annual public funeral ceremony for its war dead, *anêr agathos* denotes the brave Athenian citizen who dies fighting for his polis.[34] But *anêr agathos* is also a phrase with aristocratic connotations and origins, implying an ennobling identification with the birth-elite as opposed to a new elite based on economic wealth and commerical power or the masses (the *dêmos*) in general.

Whether you thought your Homer would make you socially

superior or simply a brave hoplite citizen, a public orator of the late fourth century emphasises the value of Homeric poetry as a moral education which encouraged his audience's forefathers to fight off the barbarians at Marathon (Lycurgus 1 [*Against Leocrates*] 102). Lycurgus goes on to quote a speech from the *Iliad* in which Hector exhorts the Trojans to be prepared to die fighting in order to defend wife, child, home and country. Unlike the alleged deserter whom Lycurgus is prosecuting, the Athenians fighting at Marathon are said to have listened to these words and acted on them by being prepared to die, not just for Athens' survival but for the whole of Greece (104). Thus, selective interpretation of Homer's heroes could be presented as fundamental to the formation of exemplary Athenian military manhood.

Ajax's close intertextual relationship with the *Iliad* actually problematises any idea that Homer's heroes are straightforwardly exemplary for the Athenian male. The play's distinctive presentation of characters from Homer actually invites its audience to reflect on the dilemmas and difficulties which underpin the question of what it is to be an *anêr agathos*. The play may give us an Ajax who is worthy of cult-worship and Demosthenic praise, but we will see that it also gives us an Ajax whose specific distortions of Homeric agency are unfriendly to fifth-century polis values in certain respects. Despite disputes over the extent of Ajax's culpability, his sanity or the extent of the play's rehabilitation of his standing, many critics have agreed that the play's meanings are generated through a confrontation between Homeric tones and positions on the one hand, and the fifth-century Athenian socio-cultural 'milieu' on the other.[35] There are scholars who would deny that *Ajax* has any significant link with the 'here and now' concerns and ideologies of democratic Athens.[36] But the *Ajax* can only make sense if its implied dialectic between Homeric 'intertext' and Athenian context is acknowledged and pursued.

An important element in this dialectic is Ajax's relationship with other heroes. In Homer, only Achilles is a better fighter than Ajax (*Iliad* 2.768-9). This traditional ranking and relationship informs our tragedy considerably. Like Achilles, favours: his majesty rests on 'lies' and his skill 'deceives with misleading tales' (23-5). If only men could have seen the truth then 'mighty Ajax, in anger over the arms would not have planted in his chest the smooth sword' (24-7). He then affirms Ajax's 'second-best' status and reflects that while death comes to all, honour belongs to those whose 'fair story' a god exalts after they die (27-33).

The Pindaric defence of Ajax's *kleos* (fame, reputation in song) gets a further twist in *Nemean* 8. Again, the ode celebrates an Aeginetan athletic victor (Deinias). The ode's main narrative deals with the Judgement of Arms and is meant to illustrate envy's power to obscure the great and the good. (The connection of this thought with Ajax's downfall is close to the Chorus's observations at *Ajax* 155-7.) Pindar observes that oblivion 'overwhelms many a man whose tongue is speechless, but whose heart is bold, in a grievous quarrel' (24-5). The 'greatest prize' has been offered up to 'shifty falsehood' and while the Greeks favoured Odysseus 'with secret votes', Ajax was stripped of the golden armour and 'wrestled with a gory death' (25-7). Pindar clearly implies that Odysseus' superior rhetorical skills and outright lies won the day. In the next stanza he is equally adamant that Ajax deserved to win the armour because he had been a better fighter than Odysseus. Ajax's sad story shows that 'hateful deception existed even long ago', that such deception is the 'companion of flattering tales' and that it 'represses what is illustrious but holds up for obscure men a glory that is rotten' (32-4). Again we have the sense that Odysseus' lies and Homer's story-telling are complicit in their denigration of Ajax. Pindar is not consistent about this complicity. In *Isthmian* 4, he again notes that Ajax's valour went unrewarded by the Greeks and that his suicide brings blame on them. But this time Pindar acknowledges that Homer has immortalised Ajax's excellence in his 'divine verses' (35-42).

None of these odes has a definite date – though many have been conjectured.[46] And much discussion of their relationship with *Ajax* has centred on whether or not *Nemean* 8's unprecedented mention of 'secret votes' thereby implies it was a source for Teucer's claim that the voting was corrupted in some way (1123).[47] We will never know for sure whether Pindar's ode influenced *Ajax* or vice versa. They may have had a common source which is lost.

Pindar's varying formulations of Ajax's story may, however, tell us something more fundamental about our tragedy's relationship with tradition. Sophocles' rendition complicates Pindar's take on the Ajax story and Homeric poetics. For the Pindaric condemnation of Odysseus is not endorsed by the play: for all their hatred and suspicion, the Sophoclean Ajax and his supporters are proved wrong about Odysseus – he is not the villain of *Nemean* 8. Indeed, it is Ajax who deploys deception in our play, not Odysseus. Ajax's anger and his arrogant attitude towards the gods also complicates the Pindaric promotion of his 'virtue'. Pindar does not speak of any divine-sent madness – a feature of Ajax's downfall in Sophocles which makes secure moral, political or religious assessment of him very difficult indeed. Furthermore, Tecmessa contributes a critique of Ajax's motivation and outlook which shows that tragedy can surpass all other genres as a forum for discussing what constitutes heroic merit.

Consciously or not, Sophocles has trumped Pindar's presentation by pointing to the complexity of 'judgement' when one moves from the arms to the man. The *Ajax* suggests that Pindar has displayed the same kind of partiality, selectivity and deceptiveness which he levels at Homer and Odysseus in *Nemean* 7 and 8. Of course, Sophocles cannot be immune from such charges either: instantiations and 'versions' of a tradition are always concealing and downplaying certain story-elements while inventing or foregrounding others. But we will see that the *Ajax* fosters and then frustrates our critical desire to form a cut-and-dried judgement about its central character's heroic worth and claims. This moral complexity betokens a kind of 'intellectual virtue' on Sophocles' part – he has presented his Ajax in a way which eschews 'bias' about his worth and which betrays an interest in foregrounding all sides of the argument about the hero's culpability, attitudes and behaviours. I will be claiming that the *Ajax* actually has something to say about the imagine Odysseus performing some expressive body language: Ajax cannot see him, but the audience can derive some irony (even humour) from watching Odysseus watching Ajax describing Odysseus as a 'villainous fox' who he will flay to death with a whip (110).[7] Ajax's responses to Athena in this brief sub-scene make it clear that he is out of his mind. But they also show that Ajax believes that Odysseus and the Atreids have dishonoured him by depriving him of Achilles' arms. He explicitly speaks in terms of loss of honour and punishment (*atimaousi*: 98, *dikên*: 113).

When Ajax becomes more lucid later in the play, he is still not ashamed of attempting to wreak vengeance on his enemies. It is his failure to succeed in his vengeance and the humiliating outcome of that failure which shames him. Like Athena, Ajax thinks it right to harm friends and hurt enemies: as several commentators note, this attitude is typical of archaic and classical Greek values and can, perhaps, be seen as the mainstay of the 'heroic code' which we can extrapolate from Homer's epics.[8] But this does not mean that Ajax's desire for vengeance is unproblematic.

After only 27 lines of dialogue with him, Athena allows the mad hero to return inside to continue torturing the animal (116-17). As he leaves, he somewhat arrogantly orders Athena 'to stand as an ally by my side'. The pathos of Ajax's predicament is enhanced by his mistaken view of the goddess as his friend and his presumptuousness in ordering a goddess around (see also 'I bid you have your way' at 112). Athena revels in her control of Ajax's perception and beliefs and it is ironic that he thinks that he has power to 'bid' her to do anything. This irony is deepened when we later learn that Ajax has angered Athena because in the past he told her to 'stand beside the other Argives: where I fight, battle will never break the line' (774-5).

The first lines of Odysseus in the prologue raise a staging difficulty: 'Voice of Athena, dearest of the gods! Your call is so familiar, even though you are out of sight' (14-15). Odysseus can hear Athena but he cannot *see* her. Is she on-stage or projecting her voice from behind the scenes? Later in this opening scene, a raving Ajax will emerge from his tent hailing Athena as if he can see her (91-2). Athena makes the frightened Odysseus invisible to Ajax (83-5). Later on, Ajax's spear-bride (Tecmessa) will describe this scene as if Ajax had been talking to nothing or else something very shadowy or murky (301-2): 'In the end he rushed through the door, and talked to some shadow.' Critics are divided on whether or not Athena is on stage during the prologue.[9] But, as one scholar remarks, 'even the selection of a particular staging for a particular production cannot finally remove the ambiguities and uncertainties of vision expressed in this opening section'.[10]

Whether we think of Athena as on-stage or off, we have the bizarre spectacle of Odysseus searching for Ajax and being addressed by a goddess who is invisible to him, followed by the harrowing appearance of a still insane Ajax who sees Athena while at the same time failing to see Odysseus because of a divine distortion of his vision. This unparalleled piece of stagecraft focuses the audience's attention on the themes of vision and madness through the tropes of physical (in)visibility. The question of what counts as sanity and the difficulty of determining Ajax's state of mind are important themes in the tragedy. This is an early example, then, of the way in which staging, action and language combine to emphasise this tragedy's powerful themes.

Pity, *sôphrosunê* and intellectual virtue (118-33)

On Ajax's exit, Athena remarks that Ajax's fall is testament to the 'greatness and strength of the gods' (118). But Odysseus expresses nothing but pity (121-6):

> I pity him in his wretchedness nonetheless, although he is my enemy, because he has been harnessed to an evil delusion; I look not to his case more than to my own. For I see that all we who live are nothing more than phantoms or an insubstantial shadow.

Odysseus' restraint and pity for Ajax is striking here, not least because it is a response to Athena's boast of divine power. When he compassionately describes Ajax as 'wretched' (*dustênon:*

importance of this principle, they say. Ironically, Ajax will call on the vital support of his sailor-chorus for the protection of his partner and son (565-71). But he requires that support as a response to his own suicide. Thus the 'great' man repays the support and loyalty of his men with an act which will end his support and protection of them for ever. We may wish to see Ajax's self-destruction as understandable and justifiable but we should note that the Chorus's exceptional fear and neediness in relation to Ajax are prominent throughout the play (134-40, 245-53, 1211-16).

It has been argued that Sophocles wishes to convey 'a particularly unheroic image of the ordinary sailors, while pulling out all the stops in evoking a Homeric image of their military and political dependence on the prowess of the single superior warrior'.[23] On this reading, the Chorus enhance Ajax's positive, if aristocratic, attributes as a leader by representing a rather pathetic image of the common man in need of guidance and paternalistic, aristocratic leadership. In the *parodos*, for example, they say that they have no strength to defend themselves without Ajax in the face of hostile clamour (165-6).

The question of whether the Chorus's apparent frailty helps to underline Ajax's positive qualities or simply adds definition to his out-datedness as a Homeric-style hero is difficult to answer – perhaps there is genuine ambiguity between these two impressions. It is also difficult to gauge the colouring of the Chorus in relation to the Athenian masses whom they must, to some extent, evoke. By this, I do not mean that the Chorus are to be seen as 'the same' as the play's audience or as automatically representative of the audience's views. Nor are they simply to be seen as interpreters of the action for the audience – the *parodos* shows that the audience knows *more* than the Chorus about the rumours concerning Ajax.[24] But the Chorus of Salaminian sailors are closer than most tragic choruses to the Athenian *dêmos* in terms of *identity*. They are 'sons of Erectheus' (202) – Erectheus was a mythical king of Athens. Ajax associates their 'native Salamis' with 'famous Athens' (859-60). And in the final lyric ode of the play, as they stand despairing beside Ajax's unburied body, the Chorus wish that they might be 'where the wooded sea-washed promontory (*prob-lêma*) stands over the sea, below the flat top of Sunium' and they might 'greet holy Athens' (1219-21). As Rose puts it, the Chorus's description 'fuses the very headland of Attica with Ajax, whom they have just called their "bulwark" (*probola*, 1212)'. At their most sympathetic moments, Ajax and the Chorus are 'most intimately and directly fused with the land and city of Sophocles' own audience'.[25]

It is not quite right to view the Chorus as a 'fundamentally degraded image ... of the Athenian *dêmos*'. Nor are they 'ideal' Athenian citizens.[26] Rather, they exhibit a mixture of positive and negative traits. In the *parodos*, as we have seen, they offer some thoughtful maxims on reciprocity. And they make some inspired, if not completely accurate, guesses as to the divine source of Ajax's malady. The Chorus may be very fearful, overly reliant on their leader and at times blind to his faults and intentions. But we will see that they also display a form of wisdom which makes them more than a spineless mob who are nothing without elite leadership.

Where the first section of the *parodos* was probably chanted, the second section was fully sung in lyric metres (172-200). This lyric section has two corresponding stanzas known as a *strophê* and *antistrophê*. In the former, the Salaminians ponder as to which of the gods has caused Ajax's downfall – they suggest Artemis and Ares. In the latter they express the hope that Zeus and Apollo will 'avert this vicious rumour' (185-6) and they reflect that if Ajax *has* really attacked the animals then he cannot be in his right mind and must have been visited by some sickness from the gods (182-5). The ode concludes with a stanza known as an epode in which the Chorus urge Ajax to 'rise up from the ground' (193). They are anxious that Ajax should defend himself against his enemies. They conclude with a striking image of those enemies' insolence (*hubris*) and 'scathing mockery' spreading like a forest-fire and fanned by the winds (196-200).

I have already discussed the *parodos* and its significant uses of Homeric language, its imagery and its point of view. For the first time, we see Ajax through the eyes of his friends rather introduced to us as having a keen mind. Sophocles is preparing us for Tecmessa's display of rationality and intelligence in her later tussle with Ajax himself.

It is not just the reflective, philosophical side to Tecmessa's intellectual virtue which shines through in this scene. The Chorus are principally relieved by the practical consequences of Ajax's return to sanity and activity: 'now that the trouble has gone there will be less talk about it' (264). By contrast, Tecmessa's ability to imagine and transmit Ajax's awakening to pain illustrates what Stanford calls her 'deeply compassionate nature'.[10]

Tecmessa had challenged Ajax as to why he was leaving the tent at midnight: 'he said little to me, only the ever-repeated words: "woman, silence adorns women." I understood and stopped while he rushed off alone.' (293-4). These reported words recall the iambic invective of the archaic poet Semonides. Semonides' 'bee woman' is the one female 'type' who is commended because she sits apart and does not gossip about sex with other women (fragment 7.91).[11] Indeed, both Athenian and non-Athenian literary texts 'universally praise female silence and verbal submission while equating women's talk with promiscuity and adultery'.[12] There is even a civic expectation that women should not talk too much or attract too much verbal attention (Thucydides 2.45.2).

Does Tecmessa signal the formulaic and prejudicial quality of these expectations by putting them in the mouth of the raving Ajax? His brusque attitude towards Tecmessa is certainly an early sign of his 'strongly male-centred conception of shame and nobility'.[13] Ajax later disparages Tecmessa's grief by condemning female lamentation in public (579-81). He even represents his (false) acceptance of her appeals as having *his* speech feminised (651).[14] Ajax finds fault with Tecmessa at nearly every turn. However, this play helps its audience to see that his 'ever-repeated' view that women should keep quiet is misplaced. Tecmessa disobeys this injunction to be silent with her efforts to dissuade him from suicide. Although she is unsuccessful, Ajax is moved by her words to make arrangements for his dependants. And we will see that her arguments provide a forceful critique of Ajax's behaviour. Tecmessa will only become mute again during the quarrel over Ajax's corpse and this in itself may be symbolic. For Ajax's journey towards suicide derives in part from the fact that he undervalues a woman's words while overvaluing masculine talk – he is always viewing his disaster in terms of what shameful things other men will say and think of him (382, 440-4, 458-80, 462-5). Ajax's self-slaughter is partly engendered by (fear and shame about) male talk and a concomitant disrespect for the discourse of women.

Tecmessa next describes Ajax's arrival back in the tent and his return to relative sanity. (In my final chapter, I will come back to the problem of determining whether or not this description allows us to determine his state of mind.) She tells us that Ajax's realisation of what he has done leads to uncharacteristic behaviour: he has been tearing out his hair and moaning (310-21). He does not moan deeply (like a 'bellowing bull') as he usually would (322). These shrill cries are not Ajaxian: 'he always considered such wailing the mark of a cowardly (*kakou*), low-spirited man' (319-20).[15] The implication here is that Ajax's mad actions have reduced him to the position of a woman. Ajax may be returning to some form of sanity but he is not himself.

Ajax's character and isolation are marked by his relationship with human language and communication in the prologue and first episode. Ajax displays faltering and often violent versions of spoken language (threats, curses, shouts); he has frequent lapses into inarticulate noises or mocking laughter; he becomes silent or is described as 'speechless'. In Tecmessa's speech his utterances are all described as groans, threats, or shouts and these are punctuated by long silences (208, 311, 312, 317). As Segal puts it, 'he vacillates between the extremes of talking big and utter silence'.[16]

When Tecmessa's long speech is over, we start to hear Ajax off-stage: he begins with groans (333, 336). He then moves to monosyllables which appeal to his young son. Next, he stutters the name of his half-brother, before finally uttering the connected sentence which the Chorus interprets as the mark of his return to sanity (344).[17] Ajax's struggle for sanity is thus also a struggle for speech. Ajax's use of, and attitude towards, with the Homeric Ajax's prayer to Zeus that he may not die in darkness but in the light (*Iliad* 17.645-7). The play's twists and turns are constantly mapped in terms of 'light-and-darkness' imagery.[22]

Ajax concludes his lyric lament by boasting of his unparalleled excellence: '... now I shall make grand (*megas*) my claim – like no other that Troy has set eyes on, of all the men who came from Greece, even though now I lie here like this, deprived of honour' (418-27). Of course, the battlefield boast is a favourite genre of self-assertion for heroes in Homer. But isn't it rather excessive?

We have seen that epic and lyric tradition represent Ajax as the best warrior *after* Achilles. Odysseus will echo this view (1341). And so, some scholars take Ajax's boast to form part of the case against him as a character: in claiming that he is the best without exception, he is implying that he is better than Achilles. This is thus one of 'several instances which could be quoted of a megalomaniac pride'.[23] Others argue that such boasting is normal for an epic hero.[24] After all, Achilles utters a similar boast in the *Iliad* (18.105-6). Furthermore, Ajax's literal claim is that Troy has never seen anyone else 'of such a sort as this'. According to Peter Rose, for Ajax to claim that he was *uniquely* great 'is subtly but importantly different from claiming explicitly to be better: in effect the claim to uniqueness confirms Homer's success in conveying precisely a sense of differentiation of character from those with whom *qua* great hero he has generic affinities'.[25] Ajax will later claim that Achilles himself, were he alive, would choose Ajax over Odysseus to inherit his arms (442-4). Rose argues that no reader of the *Iliad* would dispute this later claim and that it cancels any hint that Ajax underestimates the equally unique greatness of Achilles. In effect, Rose is attacking what has become known as a 'pietist' approach to the play – a version of which is eloquently articulated by Winnington-Ingram and which affirms Ajax as a great but impious and excessively arrogant hero. Winnington-Ingram himself described those who play down Ajax's impiety and arrogance as 'hero-worshippers' whose approach is 'methodologically unsound'.[26]

We will return to the 'hero-worshipping' and 'pietist' approaches – they enhance our picture of what makes Ajax such a complex and powerful tragic figure. But Ajax's claim to unique and special stature cannot be considered in isolation from a recognition of his uncertain state of mind – he is perhaps not quite 'himself' when he utters it and we must always take that into account.

Ajax reviews his options (430-80)

Ajax ends his lyrics with the word 'dishonoured' (*atimos*). Humiliation and loss of honour are also the keynotes of his next speech before Tecmessa and the Chorus. This is Ajax's first full-scale speech, and it heralds a greater degree of lucidity from him. Its second half has the same general form as the deliberative monologues which heroes utter in Homer's *Iliad*. And, like many of those monologues, the goal is that of 'finding an available means, under present circumstances, of acting in an honourable way'.[27] The speech begins a central debate between Ajax and Tecmessa which is only really concluded by the 'deception speech' (430-692). In this central section, the lineaments of his situation are laid out and subjected to penetrating moral scrutiny.

Ajax begins with a cry of sorrow: '*Aiai*! Who would ever have thought that my name would chime so well with my condition!' (430-1). The hero means that an exclamation of sorrow (*aiai*) could provide the etymology of his name: the Greek spelling of 'Ajax' is *Aias*. There was a common Greek belief that 'name is not a matter of convention but belongs naturally to its bearer and provides a clue to his character or destiny'.[28] Pindar, by contrast, derived Ajax's name from *aietos*, 'eagle', and Sophocles' etymology may be new (again we sense the difference between the Pindaric and tragic visions of this hero).[29]

Ajax goes on to compare his humiliation with the glorious success of his father on a previous expedition to Troy (436-41). He has performed comparable deeds to Telamon. But now he is 'ruined' and 'dishonoured by the Greeks'. Both Ajax and Teucer imagine what Telamon would think of them, question how they can return to him, and fear his disapproval and judgement (433-40, 1012-21). This formidable father constitutes Ajax's (and Teucer's) 'internalized other': 'a projected figure ... before whom the agent feels he is right to feel ashamed'.[30] But the father in tragedy is not simply or only a 'projection' of a typically Greek shame-culture. In classical Athenian culture, a citizen's legitimacy partly rests on the identity of his father and, in turn, the father is meant to be a figure of respect and authority whose honour and reputation are tied closely to the conduct and achievements of his offspring.[31] Greek myths, Homeric epic, and Attic tragedy are littered with tales of fathers who are too quick to judge and punish their sons: Theseus and Hippolytus, Phoenix and Amyntor, Bellerophon and Glaucus. Sophocles certainly wants to stress the pressure which Ajax and his brother are under with respect to their father's appraisal. But we will see that Ajax himself also plays the role of the father who expects his son to live up to his parentage. Ajax reproduces the same atmosphere of expectation and pressure which he himself is suffering under.

An exemplary warrior (and another source of pressure) from Ajax's own generation now enters his monologue: 'if Achilles were alive to reward the crown for valour in a contest for his arms, no one else would receive them before me' (441-3). This impossible scenario shows that Ajax views his humiliation as a breach of justice and friendship. But Ajax seems obsessed with his worth in relation to Achilles. This speech even echoes the Homeric Achilles' explanation of the depth of his anger and humiliation to a delegation (including Ajax himself) sent by Agamemnon (*Iliad* 9.356-416). And there is the further problem of Odysseus as a direct rival to Ajax. Ajax rails against the Atreids for allowing the prize to go to this 'evil-minded man' (445-6). Not only is Ajax measuring himself against his father and Achilles – he also has to face the fact that Odysseus has been deemed better than him. Again, we might agree that this is terribly unfair. Odysseus himself will state that Ajax was the single most excellent Greek at Troy excepting (of course) Achilles (1338). But is it really so unjust to award the armour to Odysseus? Odysseus may concede Ajax's excellence, but he does so in a successful rhetorical effort to get Ajax's body buried. And the fact that he is flexible and generous in this way means that he might represent a model of manhood and action which disrupts Ajax's calibration of heroism.

Ajax moves on to ask the classic, tragic (and very Sophoclean) question: 'what should I do now?' (457).[32] He presents his situation as a 'choice of lives' – another very Achillean trope from *Iliad* 9 and 18. Choice one is to stay at Troy but he protests that he is hated by the gods, the Greek army and even Troy itself (457-9). The implication here is that he may be punished with a humiliating death. Choice two is to 'desert the sons of Atreus' and sail back to his homeland (461-2). But he dismisses this as 'unthinkable' because he cannot face his returning to his father 'empty-handed with no victory prize, when he himself brought home the crown of glory' (464-5). Choice three is to 'storm Troy's walls, one against all, perform some great feat and then, finally, be killed' (467-8). But he rejects this option because it might 'please the sons of Atreus' (469). Eloquently and chillingly, Ajax articulates the sole remaining option (470-80):

> I must seek some such enterprise which will show my aged father that I, his son, am not by nature a coward (*asplanchos*: literally, 'lacking in guts'). It is shameful (*aischron*) for a man to wish for his life to be long if he experiences no alternation in his misfortunes. For what pleasure can day after day provide as it brings one near to or moves one back from death? I would not buy at any valuation the mortal who warms himself on empty hopes. The noble man (*ton eugenê*) should either live well (*kalôs*) or die well. You have heard my whole account.

Why wouldn't 'choice three' be good enough as a gutsy gesture of honourable death? Surely, it would be better for Ajax to die in the midst of brave one-on-one combats with Trojan heroes? Christopher Gill offers an attractive answer to this: in saying that 'option three' would 'give pleasure to the sons of Atreus', Ajax means that dying in an isolated assault would 'presuppose a framework of reciprocal risk-taking that is no longer intact'.[33]

not entirely couched in poetic and Homeric language. The word *klêrouchos* is a technical and prosaic word from contemporary politics (Thucydides 3.50.2).[38] Here, and uniquely for extant Attic drama, it is used figuratively – Ajax's mother is a 'shareholder' or 'lot-holder' of many years. This prosaic metaphor has no deep political significance. But its striking inclusion links Tecmessa's sentiments to the world of the audience.

Tecmessa goes on to say that she no longer has anything 'to look to' except Ajax. With memorable phrasing, she figures Ajax as her only 'country', her only 'wealth': all her salvation depends on him (518-20). Finally she offers a moving outline of the obligations which Ajax has incurred via a basic principle of reciprocity (520-4):

A man (*andri*) should keep it in his memory if perhaps he has enjoyed some pleasure. For it is always kindness (*charis*) which breeds kindness (*charin*); but when someone has been well treated and the recollection slips away, he could no longer be reckoned as a noble man (*eugenês anêr*).

Is it not more manly for Ajax to remember his responsibilities to his kin and obligations (sexual and familial) to Tecmessa by staying alive? Would a real man kill himself? Tecmessa uses a charged term for reciprocal action: *charis*. This word has a range of meanings: kindness, sexual and familial favour, or the gratitude which is expected for such favours and kindnesses.[39] The importance of *charis* as a social and moral idea for Sophocles' audience is brought out by Aristotle's later observation that there is a public temple to the Graces (*Charites*: the plural of *charis*) in Athens:

This is why they give a prominent place to the temple of the Graces (*Charites*) – to promote the requital of services: for this is characteristic of grace (*charis*) – we should serve in return one who has shown grace to us, and should another time take initiative in showing it.
Aristotle *Nicomachean Ethics* 1133a3-5

In line with Aristotle, Tecmessa expects Ajax to repay the *charis* she has shown towards him. She emphasises this point through word order and repetition: '*charis charin ...*' (522). Sophocles is very fond of giving his characters straight and immediate repetitions to emphasise meaning and/or lend emotional force to their words.[40] Tecmessa's repetition is called a '*polyptoton*' – this is where the endings of the repeated word vary. Tragic *polyptoton* often combines emotional intensity 'with a more intellectual emphasis on the quality or condition described'.[41] But Tecmessa's *polyptoton* also underlines a contrast with a *polyptoton* which Ajax uttered in *his* previous speech: '... am I to go to the Trojans' wall, engage them *singly* in *single* combat (*monos monois*), and perform some useful service before I die?' (466-8). The repetition of *monos* indicates Ajax's sense of being entirely on his own at this point. Tecmessa uses the same device to emphasise the fact he has important reciprocal ties and obligations – he is *not* alone and must not act as if he is.[42]

So Tecmessa underlines the appropriate nature of her rebuttal by imitating the *form* of Ajax's discourse (maxims, *polyptota*) at the same time as she alters the content. With her final two words (*eugenês anêr*), Tecmessa stresses that suicide would not be the act of a 'noble' man. As Holt puts it, 'Ajax's case for dying and Tecmessa's case for living rest on conflicting ideas of *eugeneia*'.[43] We will have to wait until the next chapter to evaluate Ajax's ultimate rejection of Tecmessa's persuasive definition of nobility. Some would argue that Tecmessa is appealing to 'quieter virtues' of cooperation and gratitude which, if heeded and followed, would do nothing to enhance Ajax's heroic excellence (*aretê*). Ajax chooses to die because the shame of living with failure and mockery outweighs the shame of deserting concubine and family.[44] Others claim that the conflict of interests that emerges between Ajax and Tecmessa leads him to 'disregard a fundamental aspect of traditional heroic values, the support and protection of dependent *philoi*'.[45] This is not completely true – Ajax *does* ensure that his dependant *philoi* ('friends', 'kin') will be protected. But Tecmessa's powerful combination of clear reasoning and emotional intelligence does suggest that 'reciprocity is an imperative which it is discreditable to ignore'.[46]

Tecmessa's appeal to *charis* is expertly directed to a man who is suffering under a sense of his own unrequited favours to the Greeks. But he ultimately ignores the appeal: his suicide mirrors the failure of his former warrior comrades to reciprocate due honour for his benefactions – failures which first drove him to attempt revenge. This mirroring is brought out by verbal echoes between Tecmessa's stress on the importance of remembering *charis* and Teucer's later claims that Agamemnon has betrayed *charis* and no longer remembers Ajax and his services (520-3, 588, 1267-9). And here we have a very real problem for 'hero-worshipping' critical approaches which seek to minimise Ajax's negative qualities. The play as a whole seems to posit some equation between Ajax's failure fully to answer Tecmessa's powerful demand for *charis* and the Atreids' failure to show *charis* to Ajax by awarding him the armour.

The sense that Tecmessa has a very good case for interrogating Ajax's definition of nobility is further enhanced by Homeric resonances.[47] Her speech closely and deliberately recasts parts of a vivid exchange in book 6 of Homer's *Iliad* in which the Trojan hero Hector converses with his wife Andromache on the ramparts of Troy (Homer *Iliad* 6.369-481). When Sophocles' Ajax goes on to demand the presence of his son and addresses him directly, this also has a deliberate resemblance to the same Iliadic scene. Having listened to Andromache's plea that he should remain in the city to fight, Hector refuses her advice but delivers a speech of great feeling for her (6.440-65). He tries to take up his child (Astyanax) into his arms. Astyanax is frightened by the plume on his father's helmet and his parents laugh. Hector puts down his helmet, picks up his son and prays for him (6.466-81). Although Sophocles makes good use of this scene in Homer, it is important to realise that he disposes it quite differently. In no sense could the Sophoclean scene be called a 'copy' of the Homeric original: rather, the recollection and 'recasting' of the Hector-Andromache episode brings a certain significance to Tecmessa's and Ajax's actions and words.

Tecmessa's speech recasts elements of Andromache's appeal to Hector *and* his reply. There is no simple correlation between Tecmessa and Homer's Andromache. Tecmessa spends much less time than Andromache in asking for pity in favour of two points which we have already outlined: (a) her relationship with Ajax and the obligations which it imposes and (b) the bad reputation which is entailed by the shameful treatment of one's abandoned dependants. Tecmessa's appeal to the second point is a clear echo of *Hector's* consolatory speech to Andromache.

Both Hector and Tecmessa imagine the direct speech of a third party and Tecmessa's 'so will he say' (504) is a version of Hector's 'so will one speak of you' (*Iliad* 6.462). But Hector's picture of Andromache's life of slavery is drawn with more detail and, crucially, he shows a husband's sympathy for his wife's predicament. Tecmessa's recasting of Hector's words generates the irony that it is *she* who has to describe her future of enslavement to Ajax rather than the other way round. And he is planning suicide, not a glorious death in battle. Tecmessa shames Ajax by turning the Homeric Hector's note of sympathy into 'a sarcastic saying by one of Ajax's enemies'.[48] Tecmessa's bitterness is enhanced by the fact that she replaces Hector's word 'wife' with the term 'concubine'. When she goes on to demand that Ajax feel shame at abandoning his parents and dependants, she is appealing to a concept which stops Hector from staying on the ramparts with Andromache. Hector is ashamed to behave like a coward in the eyes of his fellow Trojans (*Iliad* 6.442). But it is clear that Ajax will feel more shame about his humiliation before the army than he will about deserting his familial *philoi*.

In the *Iliad*, Andromache attempts to dissuade Hector from meeting Achilles in battle by imagining her isolation if he dies and Troy is captured by the Greeks (*Iliad* 6.411-32). We can compare this powerful appeal with Tecmessa's formulation (510-20): Andromache is much briefer than Tecmessa in imagining her son as an orphan but the latter is more succinct about the death of her parents and her sense of isolation. Unlike Hector, Ajax himself has destroyed his consort's 'homeland'. The difference between Tecmessa's situation and that of

Andromache is (paradoxically) marked by the intertextual similarities between their speeches: at the same time as we compare
Tecmessa to Andromache, we contrast their situations too.
With great pathos, Tecmessa points to the fact that Ajax has
taken her country from her – his suicide would leave her
without a homeland.[49]

So, Tecmessa's tone and desperation are amplified by the
recasting of an Iliadic scene. Where Hector seems understanding towards Andromache, Tecmessa points to the
harshness of Ajax. Where Hector must die on the plain to avoid
shame, Tecmessa styles Ajax's threatened suicide as a shameful
failure of reciprocity and an abrogation of his duties of care
towards his son, consort and parents.

This evocation of Troy's premier warrior and the implication
that Ajax is harsher by contrast develops even further when
Eurysaces is brought out to see his father. But it is worth
remembering that Sophocles' use of the Iliadic scene does more
than define Ajax's and Tecmessa's priorities and predicaments.
As I have already discussed, it matters that the hero of the
Homeric model is *Hector* as opposed to any other warrior: Ajax
and Teucer regard the fateful gift-exchange between Ajax and
Hector as sealing the fates of both heroes (658-66, 1024-39).
The intertextual echoes between 485-582 and *Iliad* 6.407-493
suggest that Ajax's and Hector's stories *really are* laced
together.

Father, mother and son (525-645)

Ajax responds ambiguously and coldly to Tecmessa's entreaties,
saying only that she will win his approval if she carries out his
orders. He demands to see his young son, Eurysaces. Tecmessa
explains that she put the child out of harm's way while Ajax was
raving, although she tactfully phrases this in terms which
suggest that it would have been the child's fault if he had 'met'
Ajax and been killed (533). Ajax says he approves Tecmessa's
presence of mind, but the approbation seems cold and formal.

Ajax then picks up Eurysaces and addresses him directly.
Once more, Sophocles' scene creates meaning by recasting

details of the Iliadic scene on which it is modelled (*Iliad* 6.466-85). In the touching Homeric vignette, Hector's baby son (Astyanax) is frightened (*tarbêsas*) of his father's helmet and its plume (6.468-70). Amid affectionate parental laughter, the Trojan hero discards that source of fear immediately. In our play, Ajax assumes that Eurysaces will 'have no dread' (*tarbêsei gar ou*) when he looks on his father covered in the blood of the slaughtered animals (545-6).

So there is a chilling contrast between the light-hearted atmosphere in the Homeric scene and the harshness of Ajax's words. Astyanax's fear is indulged and lovingly addressed. Eurysaces is expected to be unfazed by the sight of his father steeped in gore. Even worse, any sign of fear would mean that the boy is not 'rightly' his own (547). Ajax comes across as seriously unhinged here: he wants Eurysaces to prove his parentage by looking at the blood which signifies his father's crime and shame.

Ajax's severity continues (548-51):

He must immediately (*autika*) be broken in like a young horse in his father's savage ways (*ômois ... nomois*), and be made like him in his nature (*phusin*). My son, may you be more fortunate than your father, but in other repsects like him; you could not then be bad.

Again, these words transform their Homeric model. Hector only wishes for Astyanax to be a great warrior in the future (*Iliad* 476-81). Ajax wants Eurysaces broken in *immediately*. Hector hopes his son will be hailed as 'much better than his father' (6.479). Ajax wants his son to be luckier than he was. And yet, even as he stands there amid shameful slaughter, he thinks that Eurysaces should be the same as him in other respects. Ajax's words seem designed to provoke maximum unease in an audience. As one critic puts it, 'what sort of example does he provide for his son?'.[50] If the son is to emulate his father's nature, will he not suffer as Ajax has done? And how can the oxymoronic ascription of the adjective *ômos* (savage, raw, cruel) to the noun *nomos* (way, law, custom, rule) signal that Ajax is a straightforward role model? 'Rawness' (*ômotês*) connotes excessiveness, barbarity and an uncivilised nature.[51] 'Custom' (*nomos*) is also charged, implying as it does (in fifth-century Athens) the rule of law and social contract or the domination of culture, tradition and nurture over nature – it is the opposite of the untamed savagery connoted by *ômotês*. By putting these opposites together, Ajax signals his difficult relationship with community and social harmony, and he does so in language which speaks to, and yet marks his distance from, the civic culture of the audience.

Ajax does soften momentarily to imagine Eurysaces as a child: 'fed by the light breezes, nurturing your young soul, a joy to your mother here' (557-8). But this brief moment of tenderness towards Tecmessa is purloined from Homer's Hector (*Iliad* 6.481). And Ajax quickly darkens the mood again by issuing instructions concerning what is to be done after his suicide. The Chorus are to protect Eurysaces and convey the message to Teucer that he must act as Eurysaces' guardian. Eurysaces is to look after Ajax's parents in their old age. Cruelly, Ajax says nothing about what is to become of Tecmessa.

Ajax goes on to bequeath his shield to Eurysaces – the son is to inherit the wide *sakos* from which he gets his name (575-8). Was the shield actually there on stage? We cannot know.[52] This huge piece of equipment, 'made of the hides of seven bulls', is described in anachronistic terms which evoke the hoplite shields which were wielded by many of the citizens watching the play. These shields were also part of the armour supplied by the polis to the orphans of Athenian citizens killed in battle. We saw that the orphans paraded in this armour in a preplay ceremony at the Great Dionysia. Goldhill has shown how Ajax's scene with Eurysaces must be framed with this ideologically-charged ceremony as well as its Homeric intertext:

The scene of Ajax with his child, juxtaposed with the preplay ceremony of the orphans in military uniform, significantly alters the way we look both at Sophocles' tragedy and at the notion of a child, at offering advice and a role model to a child. The context for understanding this scene goes beyond its instantiation in a performance in the theatre, beyond its interrelations with Homer. This scene cannot fully be appreciated or understood without realizing the complex interplay of its writing with the ideology of the fifth-century *polis* of Athens.

Goldhill, 'Great Dionysia', p. 118

Ajax's advice and bequest evince his extremism and make him a problematic role model. But because the state educates and equips its war-orphans to fill their fathers' places in the hoplite rank (and celebrates that process in the theatre), the contrast between the scene and the ceremony underlines Ajax's incompatibility with Athens' collective military ideology.

Ajax instructs Tecmessa to take herself and the boy inside and forbids her to weep in lamentation before their tent: 'a woman is indeed a creature most prone to wail' (580). He uses imagery which ominously signals his intention to use a blade against himself: 'it is not for a wise doctor to lament with incantations over a disease that calls for the knife' (581-2). Tecmessa pleads with Ajax to be persuaded and to 'soften' (594). But her entreaties are met with his countering instructions not to question her, to 'exercise self-control' (*sôphronein*), to cease talking or to talk to others who will listen, and simply to go inside quickly, shutting the door behind her (585-94). Like Athena (and the Atreids later), Ajax glosses *sôphrosunê* as obedience and a curbing of dissenting speech.[53] Ajax's and Tecmessa's increasing agitation is signalled by the way in which their countering responses fill only half of one iambic line (591-4). Ajax's final words are chilling (594-5): 'It seems to me that you are thinking foolishly if even now you plan to educate (*paideuein*) my character (*êthos*)'. Here, the hero self-consciously acknowledges his unalterable nature; this is a proclamation which makes his apparent change of mind in his next speech all the more surprising.

Many critics believe that Ajax is still sitting on the *ekkuklêma* at this point and is now withdrawn into the tent. Tecmessa and Eurysaces follow him in as the Chorus begin their first *stasimon* (596-645). That way, the audience are led to

72

expect a shriek of anguish from Tecmessa as Ajax kills himself in front of her and off-stage.[54] Ajax's re-entry at 646 then comes as a real surprise. Some scholars have worried that this surprise is diminished in its effect if Tecmessa follows him out of the same door. Thus they posit a second door for the 'woman's quarters' which she and Eurysaces go through (and re-enter from at 646), or else argue that she remains on stage.[55] We cannot even be sure that *any* of the three characters exit at this point. But it is hard to imagine that Tecmessa does not exit given Ajax's repeated demand that she go through a door. And the greatest dramatic impact seems to follow from an exit by all three through the same door.

The first *stasimon* develops themes which have already been expressed in the play and which the third *stasimon* will reprise (596-645, 1185-221).[56] The *parodos'* disjunction between the Chorus' knowledge and the audience's experience of Ajax has gone. The Chorus now realise that Ajax is a 'man past curing, stricken with madness sent by the gods' (609-12). Of course, Ajax's current state of mind is not as delusional as it was under Athena's immediate control, but the Chorus are now seeing his desire for suicide as god-sent 'madness' too. Although 'he was a powerful man in the heat of battle' he now 'keeps his thoughts' flock in loneliness and grieves his friends' (614-16). His 'greatest achievements are gone'. The Chorus *had* seen Ajax's desire for suicide as true to his mind (481-2). Now they figure his brooding isolation and introspection as abnormal. And where Ajax has just figured his *êthos* as fixed and unchangeable, they argue that he 'no longer remains constant to the temperament he grew up with but has become a stranger to it' (639-40). Ajax has gone inside himself and, at the same time, *outside* his normal social and psychological self. This contrast with Ajax's self-conception and the difficulty of determining how far Ajax is (in control of) himself throughout the scene with Tecmessa prepare us for the ambiguities of the deception speech.

5

Deception and Suicide

The problem with the deception speech

When the Chorus has finished its first *stasimon*, Ajax re-enters from his tent. His subsequent speech makes it clear that he is carrying his sword (658). Tecmessa and the Chorus are listening (652, 691). This speech is often called the 'deception speech' by critics (sometimes they use the German word 'Trugrede'). The main reason for this is that Tecmessa and the Chorus clearly interpret Ajax's words as amounting to a change of mind – he will give up his former stubbornness, will not kill himself after all and will reconcile with the Atreids and the gods (715-18, 743-4, 803-12). But, of course, he does go on to do the deed and prays that the Furies will wreak vengeance on the Atreids and the entire army (835-44). Gellie sums up the resulting critical problem: 'Ajax cannot change and Ajax cannot lie. If Ajax cannot change he speaks to deceive; if Ajax cannot lie, he is recording an honest change of heart.'[1]

When the messenger makes her realise that Ajax is still intent on suicide, Tecmessa explicitly says 'I have come to realise that I have been deceived by the man and cast out from my former favour (*charis*)' (807-8). But if Tecmessa means that Ajax's speech was *intentionally* deceptive, not every scholar has wanted to agree with her.[2] To some, it has seemed 'out of character' for Ajax to lie with intent: 'The character of Ajax is Achillean; it may be all too easily tempted to extremes of violence but not to deceit'.[3] To get round this apparent problem, Knox and Sicherl have argued that until Ajax explicitly addresses Tecmessa and his marines at 685ff., his speech is a soliloquy – he is talking reflectively to himself but being *over-*

74

heard by the other on-stage characters and the actual audience.[4] Tecmessa and the Chorus then gain a false impression because they hear what they want to hear rather than being the dupes of an active attempt to deceive them.

Knox is perhaps right to dismiss the argument that Ajax has to resort to lies so that he can commit suicide alone – this powerful and frightening hero is perfectly capable of commanding his followers to leave him be. But he might lie to relieve Tecmessa from her present anguish. We could conceive of Ajax's deception speech as a 'noble lie' which brings temporary relief to his supporters.[5] And the view that lying would be uncharacteristic of this hero starts to look very weak when we remember how much has already been made of the fact that Ajax has not been acting like 'himself' anyway. Furthermore, he has already resorted to Odyssean tactics: his night attack on the Atreids was an example of crafty (*dolios*) behaviour (47). We may agree that this behaviour is a 'total negation of heroism as Ajax has understood it in the past'.[6] But Ajax's adoption of cunning and deception can then be a warped attempt to show that he can be Odyssean too if that is what wins prizes. Perhaps we are simply meant to mark the paradox that he has to adopt the methods usually associated with his enemy in order to recover his honour.[7]

Ultimately, it is no more possible to disprove Knox's thesis that Ajax does not intend to deceive than it is to prove that a particular intention grounds the misleading impression he conveys. (We will soon encounter the view that Sophocles deliberately makes Ajax's intention opaque). But it is important that Tecmessa connects her belief that she has been misled with a failure in reciprocity on Ajax's part (807-8). Even if Ajax thinks he is doing the right thing, he *has* left her with a false impression and that failure to be clear about his intentions must be seen as a breach of the *charis* which she believes she is owed.

A second reason for calling the speech a 'deception' is that Ajax's words clearly operate ambiguously: on the surface he seems to be saying that he has changed his mind and will go to the sea-shore to cleanse himself. But we will see that his language and phrasing signal another darker plan to an attentive audience. A third reason for viewing the speech as in some sense dishonest involves the opacity of its reflections concerning yielding, alternation, *sôphrosunê* and the mutability of friendship. For example, and as we will see, elements of style, language, phrasing and juxtaposition of ideas all suggest that Ajax's statement that he will now learn self-control (*sôphronein*) is sarcastic and insincere (677-8).

The lack of critical consensus on whether or not Ajax is deceptive in these three senses is striking. Nor is there much agreement on exactly how Ajax's apparent 'insights' (however sincerely they are held) affect our reading of the play as a whole. The deception speech is 'one of the greatest problems of Sophocles, and anything anyone says about it is bound to be controversial'.[8] The ensuing analysis of Ajax's words will give a flavour of the wide range of (often incompatible) views which they have provoked. We can map the speech onto various definitions of tragedy or tragic heroism, but there is nothing quite like it in the rest of the extant tragic plays and fragments.[9] Its uniqueness and the beauty of its poetry are a testament to Sophocles' originality of vision.[10]

Womanly words and the 'softened' sword (646-65)

Ajax's speech starts as follows (646-53):

> Long and immeasurable time brings forth all things that are obscure and when they have come to light hides them again; there is nothing that is beyond expectation, but even the terrible (*deinos*) oath falls into time's power, and minds which are too strict (*periskeleis phrenes*). For even I, who at that time was terribly firm (*ta dein' ekarteroun*) like iron hardened by dipping (*baphêi sidêros hôs*), have been softened like a woman in my speech (*ethêlunthên stoma*), thanks to this woman here; I pity her that I should leave her a widow with my enemies and my son an orphan.

The idea that time has a power to reveal what is hidden and to destroy or control events is very Sophoclean, as is the related notion of cyclical alternation in the natural and social worlds which emerges at 669-76.[11] On the surface, Ajax is making the conventional poetic point that anything is possible and the most unexpected things can come to pass.[12] Overturned oaths and changed minds are appropriate images because the man who previously asserted the immutability of his *êthos* is now saying that his pity for Tecmessa and Eurysaces has changed him. An extended metaphor of metal-working conveys his previous harshness: he was hardened like hot iron that has been dipped in cold water. And the language used to describe his former firmness recalls earlier descriptions of Ajax (205, 312). Now Tecmessa has caused him to be 'feminised' in his speech. *Stoma* is ambiguous: its literal meaning is 'mouth' but it can mean the edge or point of an implement (especially a sword) and this continues the metal-working metaphor.[13] Thus we have a literal meaning, 'feminised in mouth', and a metaphorical meaning, 'softened in edge'. The idea that his speech/edge has been softened recalls the image of the doctor's knife and Tecmessa's plea that he 'be softened' (582-4, 594). But it also draws us towards Ajax's own sense that his destiny is bound up with the blade which he is currently brandishing – the gift from his friend-enemy Hector.

Ajax implies that he will not commit suicide after all – at any rate, this is the most obvious surface meaning. Is he sincere in his expression of pity? Even though he goes on to kill himself, it does not follow that he is being false: he can pity his partner and son precisely because he is going to leave them. But how deep can his pity be if he ends up destroying himself in spite of Tecmessa's entreaties? One senses that Sophocles wanted to make it difficult for his audience to gauge Ajax's state of mind here – critics have certainly been divided.[14] This is just one example of the way in which the deception speech provokes reassessment in an audience once it has gained the hindsight of Ajax's suicide. Indeed, it is crucial to view the speech from two perspectives: there is the response which an audience develops as it listens to Ajax's words (suspecting the worst) and then there is the reassessment it makes once the worst suspicions are confirmed and those same words are recalled. As for Ajax's profession of pity, his apparent genuineness perhaps becomes increasingly questionable – the more his words hint at an unchanged suicidal intent, the less we are sure of his sincerity.

Ajax's imagery does more than profess a sudden change of heart. Time and lucidity have led him to recognise that he has been capable of uncharacteristic behaviour. David Cohen argues that if Ajax kills himself amidst the carnage which marks his disgrace with the very sword which he used in this mad and angry attack, he will be 'reaffirming that unheroic, dark side of his nature which the sword represents'.[15] 'In other words,' continues Cohen, 'Ajax realises the unheroic quality of his madness and the part of his nature which produced it.' The sword he got from Hector has come to be an instrument and symbol of this madness and his unheroic side. And his first words express this insight: 'he has learnt that "nothing is beyond expectation"... not even an unheroic potential within what he had previously considered his inflexible noble *ēthos*'.[16] On this reading, Ajax's subsequent statement that he will bury his sword and the fact that he does kill himself with it are part and parcel of a process whereby he re-establishes his heroic identity and turns away from an unheroic death amid slaughtered animals by 'reinterpreting the sword and what it represents, making it an enemy, the gift of an enemy, and not his own'.[17]

Ajax may be planning an heroic death, but in the first few lines of the deception speech he *seems* to be relenting in his desire to die. However, his next set of statements would give an attentive audience some suspicion that all is not well (654-64):

Well, I shall go to the bathing-place (*loutra*) and the meadows by the shore, to wash away my defilement (*lutham'*) and escape from the heavy anger of the goddess; I shall go to where I can find an untrodden place and I shall hide (*krupsō*) this sword of mine, the most hateful of my weapons, digging it in the ground where nobody shall see it; let night and Hades keep it safely down below. For ever since I received it in my hand as a gift from Hector, I have never had anything good from the Argives.

On the surface, Ajax is saying that he will go to the shoreline of Troy and engage in some form of (ritual or non-ritual) bathing in order to wash away the blood of the slaughter, perhaps to expiate his killing of the livestock and herdsmen and to make his peace with Athena. Whether or not he is actually seeking atonement or reconciliation with the goddess is debatable.[18] Because it was a Greek custom to bury sacrificial or polluted objects, he wants to hide the sword (the instrument of his disgrace) in the ground. So far, so good. But the phrasing, syntax and the vocabulary are ambiguous and thus suggest another level of meaning.[19]

First, Ajax's word for 'bathing-place' is almost always used in Sophocles for the washing of a corpse before burial. It is used again by Teucer for the washing of Ajax's corpse (1405). Secondly, when he says he will 'hide' his sword in the ground, he uses a verb which is regularly used for the burial of a corpse. And again, this verb is used of Ajax's own burial by the Chorus (1040). What Ajax might *really* mean, then, is that he will hide the sword in his own body by fixing it in the ground and falling onto it. And this is exactly what does happen – Tecmessa later echoes Ajax's language when she describes his body as 'folded around his hidden sword' (*kruphaiôi phasganôi*: 899). His own body will be the sword's grave. When he hopes that 'night and Hades will keep the sword safely down below', he hints that the sword will be buried with him in his grave. This recalls his earlier desire to be buried with all his arms except the shield (577).

I am assuming that the external audience notice that Ajax is using ambiguous language – and that they can suspect his true intentions (to leap on his sword alone by the shore). At the same time, these words give Tecmessa and the Chorus a very different impression. But, regardless of whether or not Ajax is *intentionally* deceiving them, his words convey something more than the mere statement of what action he will take next. The sword is one of the key symbols in that deeper meaning.[20] The hostility of the sword and its donor are stressed for reasons we have already gone into. The fact that Ajax never had any benefit from the Argives since he received the sword as a gift from his 'worst enemy' (Hector) leads him to generalised reflection: 'True is men's proverb, that the gifts of enemies are no gifts and bring no benefit' (664-5).[21] This idea will be developed by Ajax in his death speech and is picked up by Teucer as he laments over Ajax's impaled body (815ff., 1024-39). We are in the first stages of a developing representation whereby his suicide becomes a completion of Ajax's single combat with Hector. By making the sword the cause of his downfall and by personifying it as an enemy slayer (663, 815ff., 1026), Ajax and Teucer want to represent the suicide as a death wrought by external forces, namely the revenge of Hector and the contrivance of the gods.

Ajax's attempt to assimilate his suicide with heroic endeavour does not go unchallenged. Just because the sword has become the instrument of an heroic enemy *for Ajax* and just because it has lost its identity as a weapon used in a shameful night attack *for him* does not mean that he can completely shake off the sinister and shameful features of his character which emerged at the beginning of the play. Ajax's language of heroic death is later countered by Menelaus' representation of Ajax as a murderous enemy who has surpassed the Trojans by 'plotting to destroy' his own comrades 'by the spear' under the cover of darkness (1054-6). Despite his vileness, Menelaus has a good point here. It is noticeable that Menelaus represents Ajax as armed with a spear as opposed to the sword (contrast 10 and 658). It is as if Menelaus is changing the weapon used in order to dispense with the complications of agency and symbolism to which previous talk (and imagery) of Hector's sword has given rise.

Yielding, alternation, friendship and enmity (666-92)

Ajax directly connects the proverb about enemies' gifts being no gift at all with his next sentence: 'Therefore (*toigar*) we shall know in future to yield (*eikein*) to the gods and we shall learn to reverence (*sebein*) the sons of Atreus. They are rulers so one ought to yield (*hupeikteon*)' (666-8).[22] One expects a sincerely-motivated Ajax to say that he will reverence the *gods* and yield

5. Deception and Suicide

to the *Atreids* rather than the other way round. Certainly, *sebein* is usually applied to gods rather human rulers.[23] Gill argues that Tecmessa's speech has not explored 'what it would mean in practical or ethical terms, for Ajax to be allowed to continue to act as protector of his *philoi* (dependants)' after his failed attempt on the lives of the Greek leaders.[24] On this reading, lines 666-8 give a graphic, but not wholly implausible picture of what this would involve, at the same time as their tone indicates how unacceptable it would be *really* to accede to Tecmessa's wishes.

The suspicion that Ajax is being in some sense insincere or sarcastic is enhanced by the fact that he says 'we shall *know*' and 'we shall *learn*' – it is as if Ajax is telling us what new lesson he knows he is expected to derive from his humiliation rather than expressing any genuine or emotional change of outlook. Furthermore, a reference to 'the future', and the future tenses which Ajax uses, suggest a crucial ambiguity. For his on-stage audience, Ajax is saying that he will be self-controlled, reverent and obedient towards the gods and the army's high command. But insofar as *we* suspect that Ajax will kill himself soon, these future tenses carry a rather different meaning: it is only true that he will end his hostility towards the Atreids and yield to the gods in the sense that a *dead* man will no longer be in a position to oppose either his divine or his human enemies.[25] Furthermore, when Ajax tells us what he *will* learn and know (666-7, 677), these futures and the rhetorical questions of his possible future knowledge are 'set in tension with his future actions and future expressions'.[26] Ajax *will* kill himself and curse the Atreids with extreme vehemence and hatred: if he really has had some profound new insight into the need for moderation and humility, then his subsequent language and behaviour will manifestly contradict it. Such a contradiction need not be inexplicable – see Seaford's arguments below – and is certainly not a clinching argument for the view that Ajax *must* be insincere at 666-8. But the striking style and tone of 'this gloriously over-stated assertion' suggest strongly that Ajax is sarcastically presenting us with the unacceptable image of submission which is entailed by staying alive.[27]

Ajax expands on the professed necessity of 'yielding' to gods and rulers by returning to the imagery and analogy of cyclical alternation:

> For even things that are terrible (*ta deina*) and very strong (*ta karterôtata*) yield to what is held in honour (*timais*); first, winters which cover the roads with snow give way to summer with its lovely fruit; and the eternal rotation of the night withdraws for day with its white horses to kindle its light; and the breath of terrible winds puts to sleep the groaning sea; moreover the omnipotent Sleep releases when it has fettered, and what it has caught it does not hold for ever. Then how shall *we* not learn good sense (*sôphronein*)? I shall; for at this late hour I understand that our enemy (*echthros*) is to be hated only to the extent that he will later become our friend (*philêsôn*), while as far as a friend is concerned I shall want to serve and help him only so far, believing that he will not always so remain. For to most mortals the haven of comradeship is not to be trusted (669-83).

There are clear parallels between this meditation on alternation and change and early Greek cosmology. For example, Anaximander speaks of opposites which pay 'penalty (*dikên*) and retribution (*tisin*) to each other for their injustice according to the assessment of Time' (12 A9 D-K). The idea here is that the observable world (cosmos) is paradoxically maintained as just and ordered by the 'strict reciprocal nature of injustice'.[28] Each successive state of cosmic dominance (e.g. heat in the summer) is compensated for by the encroachment of an opposing rival (e.g. the cold of winter). Thus we have a 'just' and ordered seasonal cycle coming from hostile and 'unjust' oppositions.

One thrust of the cosmic imagery used here is that negative, hostile, dark or fruitless phenomena give way to positive, benign, bright and fertile ones. And hence, as a corollary, Ajax's former rigidity and terrible wrath will now yield to *sôphrosunê* and the authority of the Atreids and the gods. But it is not clear that Ajax really accepts this corollary or that he can 'yield' in accordance with it. He could be saying that opposites are irreconcilable as much as they are alternating: just as there is no place for winter or night where there is summer or day, there is no place for Ajax in the land of the living where one must yield to foes.[29] And just as calm seas follow stormy ones, the calm comes before a storm, and so on. By the same logic, nobody – not even a sincere, 'yielding' Ajax – can stay 'soft' for ever. It is hard to know for sure what Ajax is getting at here; if we think he is saying that he will yield, we cannot be certain that he really means it.

As with previous lines, we sense sarcasm in Ajax's question: 'how shall we not learn good sense (*sôphronein*)?'.[30] Again, Ajax may be saying that acceding to Tecmessa's wishes would involve him becoming 'self-controlled' or 'sensible' (*sôphrôn*) in a way which he finds unacceptable. One facet of this unacceptability lies in the connotation of 'submitting to another's judgement and authority' which *sôphrosunê* is sometimes given elsewhere in the play.

It is also possible to take Ajax's words about friendship to be sarcastic and scornful. When he says 'I understand that our enemy is to be hated only to the extent that he will later become our friend' it sounds like 'the supreme – ironic – revelation of the mind of Ajax through the expression of its reverse'.[31] On this reading, Ajax concludes that if a friendship or an enmity must be qualified and limited then it must also be the case that friends can never be trusted fully. Ajax echoes the sententious and aristocratic elegy of Theognis when he complains that there is no sure 'haven of companionship' – and there is the suggestion that Hades will be the only true haven for Ajax now.[32] If he *is* distancing himself from accepting a world where 'the haven of friendship' is untrustworthy, it is easy to give an account of why this should be so: 'a world in which friends and enemies change places and the old heroic code of "Harm your enemies, help your friends" is no sure guide, is no world for Ajax'.[33] We might add that 'help friends, harm enemies' is not *just* an 'old heroic code' but a very widely-held ethic in fifth-century Greek poleis.

Ajax's 'insight' that hatred and friendship are mutable is close to Odysseus' arguments at the beginning and end of the play – Odysseus does not want to hate the hero as much as Athena and the Atreids would wish, and he sees the value of now acting like a *philos* (friend) to Ajax by offering his corpse respect and honour and insisting on his burial (121-6, 1332-45, 1359). Ajax's Odyssean 'insight' into the mutability of *philia* (friendship, kinship) thus continues the deception speech's contrast with his previous uncompromising attitudes, not to mention its various parallels with the 'softer' outlooks of Tecmessa, Odysseus and the Chorus.[34]

In saying that enemies can turn into friends, and vice versa, Ajax echoes a maxim attributed to Bias of Priene – a sixth-century thinker who was one of the 'seven sages'. The sentiment gets recycled frequently in later texts and is often used to convey the cynical idea that friends are unreliable and hence that one's commitment to them should be qualified. Above all, Ajax is dwelling on the idea that his own friends in the Greek army have become his enemies. But, in a sense (and ironically), Ajax *himself* has succumbed to the mutability of friendship. He has attacked his former allies and will (to an extent) violate his obligations to *philoi* like Tecmessa and the Chorus who have remained loyal. So, Ajax may be admitting that he has himself been swept along by mutability even as he scorns its implications.

In echoing the deception speech's sentiments of mutability, Odysseus will later use them to secure Ajax's burial. But Teucer assumes that Ajax is intractable even after death. This assumption perhaps suggests that the hero is *articulating* the 'insight' of 'mutability' but not *accepting* it. Certainly, his final death speech will reassert the permanence of his hatred towards the Atreids (835-44). Thus, Ajax's 'insight' into mutability is perhaps one of the means by which an Athenian audience (paradoxically) forms a negative appraisal of the hero: he cannot put aside his pride or his sense of honour and injustice by embracing change and flexibility.

But many commentators, Christopher Gill being a recent example, side with Ajax here: he sees the Bias maxim as unacceptable precisely *because* it can be used to excuse the injustice, ingratitude and dishonour done to him when the arms of Achilles were awarded to Odysseus.[35] The Atreids' failure to award him the arms is incompatible with the principles of fairness and reciprocity that should be present within a properly conducted friendship. In a treatise about rhetoric, Aristotle argues that the Bias maxim characterises the qualified and negative attitude of old men in general and their lack of trust towards others in particular (*Rhetoric* 1389b23-5). So Aristotle sees the maxim as a commonplace but he casts it in a negative light. When discussing the value of maxims to the rhetorician, Aristotle refers to Bias' sentiment once again. He is arguing that an orator can deploy maxims which contradict 'the most popular sayings' (such as 'know thyself' and 'nothing in excess'): 'one's character would appear better, if one were to say that it is not right, as men say, to love as if one were bound to hate, but rather to hate as if one were bound to love ... or thus, "The maxim does not please me, for the true friend should love as if he were going to love for ever"' (Aristotle *Rhetoric* 1395a26-31).

Aristotle is testifying to the Bias maxim as a precept which has common currency. But he also shows how easily it can be pulled apart by the countering notion that friendship should be permanent and immutable. It is also noticeable that Aristotle thinks a good impression can be created by the speaker who endorses one half of the maxim without the other: qualified enmity is a good thing, while qualified friendship is not. Of course, an entire century could separate the writing of *Ajax* and the *Rhetoric*. But he does at least show us that a sarcastic rejection of the maxim as a guide to life on the part of Ajax is not idiosyncratic or unreasonable by the lights of the classical period.

The ambiguous form of Ajax's language makes it very hard for us to pin down his attitude to mutability. It is tempting to follow Winnington-Ingram's pietism in thinking that Ajax now fully understands mutability while having none of it himself because of his pride.[36] That way, we can reconcile the clearly profound quality of his words with the hints of sarcasm. But such understanding and rejection of mutability cannot really be made compatible with Gill's idea that Ajax's suicide is an exemplary and heroic gesture which points up the negative aspects of 'mutability' in the sphere of *philia*.

Another position which runs counter both to Gill's brand of 'hero-worshipping' and Winnington-Ingram's pietism is that Ajax's insight into 'mutability' is genuine (rather than scornful or sarcastic) and is completely compatible with his determination to die. The most complicated version of this position is that of Richard Seaford and we must now devote some space to his approach. Seaford agrees with others that 'throughout Ajax intends to kill himself, that what he says in the speech is ambiguous ..., that his hearers in the drama (as opposed to the audience) perceive only the surface meaning, and that although his speech does deceive them into believing that he has decided to live, its primary (or only purpose) is to express a new insight'.[37] So the name of the game is to work out what this insight is and to explain its 'half-concealed' nature.

A crucial element of Seaford's explanation is the intersection between Ajax's opaque language and the riddling, antithetical discourse of the pre-Socratic philosopher Heraclitus. In turn, Heraclitus' style and content are influenced by a discourse of mystic initiation.[38] In Athens, initiation into the mysteries was a central religious ritual in the life of a citizen. Where I have been discussing Ajax's remarks on changeability in terms of Anaxamandrian 'alternation', Seaford thinks that they draw on the mystic-Heraclitean insight that nothing is permanent except change and that everything is converted by time into its opposite. Thus, Ajax's imagery of bathing and shrouding recalls the mystic interpenetration of life and death: the imagined, symbolic death of a mystic initiand brings death into life, but it also, inasmuch as the ritual overcomes death, brings life into death. But of course Ajax's 'life in death' will involve *real* death. On the ethical level, the deception speech posits the insight of the interpenetration of friendship and hostility via the ambiguity of Hector's sword. This sword was a gift which originally marked a relationship of *xenia* (guest-friendship) but it 'reacquires the original hostility of its donor, and yet in a further reversal is to become most favourable (in bringing death)'.[39]

Ajax's mystic-Heraclitean principle of 'interpenetration', where amity becomes enmity and so on, is actually different from the principle underlying reciprocity, whether it be the positive reciprocity of gift-exchange and *charis* or the negative reciprocity of absolute hostility and vendetta. The reasoning is complex and the evidence is wide-ranging, but Seaford sees the mystic rituals of Athens and Heraclitean thought as analogous to legal and economic changes which we associate with the emergence of the polis and the rituals used to promote communality in the Athenian polis in particular (hero-cult, mystery-cult, Dionysian festival and theatre). And this is where the *Ajax* fits into Seaford's wider theory of the relationship between tragedy and Athens as a developing city-state.

First, Ajax's cosmic and social insight into yielding and interpenetration means he must limit his hostility and all interpersonal reciprocal action generally. This insight entails the exercise of *sôphrosunê* (677). The parallels with Heraclitus' fragments suggest that this definition of *sôphrosunê* as the antithesis of interpersonal reciprocity is being seen (by Sophocles and Heraclitus) as the basis of communality in the polis. Secondly, the insight means that Ajax prioritises communality and rejects household solidarity. In this, he is similar to the Hector of *Iliad* 6, and we saw how important that Homeric parallel was for understanding Ajax's exchange with Tecmessa. But, unlike Homer's Hector, the mysterious communal claim on Ajax is that he must become the focus of collective cult.

Drawing on parallels between this speech and a speech in *Oedipus at Colonus* which explicitly prefigures its protagonist's cult, Seaford argues that the deception speech's mystic-Heraclitean elements also betoken the language and functioning of hero-cult in general and Ajax's cult in particular. For example, at the end of the speech, Ajax asks the Salaminian Chorus to 'perform with honour' the same things for him as Tecmessa does (687-8). Their response is a phrase associated with the mysteries: 'I thrill with rapture' (*ephrix' erôti*: 693). Thus, Ajax's ritualised, mystic language initiates the process by which the play stages his transition from living hero to the object of cult worship after his death. And significantly, cult worship of Ajax will be *perpetual*: the permanence of collective worship provides an image of communality which counteracts the changeful unreliabilities of interpersonal relations and reciprocities.

Ajax's riddling language of interpenetration means that he has a genuine mystical insight into the changeability of all relations, whether hostile or friendly. Thus he rejects excessive hostility *and* the kind of friendly reciprocity which Tecmessa demands at 522. He is isolated from his family and relationships with other warriors because he can see that reciprocity and instability are intertwined. Seaford argues that mystery cult, hero-cult and the tragic theatre which (he believes) emerges from them are 'politically significant' because they bring non-kin around a 'single focus of emotion'.[40] Thus, hero-cult embodies a communal feeling which transcends claims from family and household as well as claims of personal reciprocity. If Ajax's insight constitutes his isolation from the same claims, then the deception speech is his 'first step' towards becoming the focus of communal cult.

It might be objected that Ajax does not go on to limit his hostility in a manner that is consistent with Seaford's reading: he curses the Atreids and invokes the 'eternal Furies' against the entire army (835-44). Seaford's answer to this apparent inconsistency essentially relies on his interpretation of Athenian hero-cult as having a 'dual role'. On the one hand, hero-cult unites Athenian citizens in 'mutual respect' rather than reciprocal hostility. On the other, hero-cult 'also deploys the hero's justified anger against Athens' enemies, and this it is ... that requires the piteous death of Ajax and his cursing of the Dorian Atreidai'.[41] For Menelaus is a Spartan ruler, and for most of the latter half of the fifth century, the Spartans were Athens' enemies. In celebrating Ajax's sad death in fifth-century cult (and in our play), Athenians may have imagined Ajax's anger as now directed at the Atreids' Spartan descendants. His value as a *permanent* focus of cult worship is as a figure who fosters communal bonds as well as one who represents wrath towards his (and Athens') foes. Thus the 'inconsistency' in the play between the deception speech and Ajax's curse is in fact an expression of the dual role of his hero-cult.

If Seaford is right, then the *Ajax* has hero-cult's social and political significance inscribed within its most beautiful and mysterious poetry. Though he does not make its implications very explicit, Seaford's reading strikes a blow against those who wish to 'depoliticise' this play (and tragedy generally) by making 'high poetry' and 'politics' mutually exclusive.[42] The idea that tragedy cannot be 'political' *because* it is so poetic and timeless-sounding is turned on its head. Ajax's insight is his passport to a permanent and stable relationship with community. The aesthetic qualities and political significance of his words are one and the same thing – they cannot be divorced from each other.

Seaford's case is powerful. For him, the ambiguities and uncertainties surrounding Ajax (how sane? how justified? how hubristic?) must be a function of the cult hero's double status as protector and object of appeasement. Ultimately, Seaford's Ajax is completely rehabilitated through cult. But is tragedy so firmly in the service of Athens' religious rituals? Is the deception speech only concerned with isolated cultic insight? What about all those uncertainties of tone and hints of sarcasm? While Seaford shows brilliantly that *Ajax* articulates the functions and ambiguities of its hero's cult status, it is not clear that Ajax's problematic qualities and ambiguous intentions are thereby completely contained and explained. For example, we might want to see the play as refiguring hero-cult's dual role as insoluble contradiction: can hero-cult *really* manage the tension between communality and private anger successfully? We will soon see that Ajax's invocation of the vengeful Furies is peculiarly extreme in its articulation. That extremity of hatred may not be as unproblematic as Seaford wants it to be.

Like Seaford, W.B. Stanford also argued for Ajax's 'insight' being genuine. But his thesis was a lot simpler: Ajax's conversion to mutability represents a new humility on his part. His failure and death, when viewed from the cosmic perspectives outlined at 671-5 are just part of the universe's harmonious cycle of events rather than 'unique personal humiliations'.[43] On this reading Ajax's suicide does not 'contradict' Ajax's sublime and philosophical insights into change and 'yielding'. Rather, his suicide is simply a form of humility which marks the dissolution of his former harshness.

It can also be argued that Ajax genuinely sees himself as yielding to the gods and the Atreids on the grounds that his death would be a form of positive reciprocity towards Athena and his own family.[44] Through his death he pays a debt he owes to Athena – she is angry with him for rejecting her (112-13, 770-7). Ajax also hopes that his death will be a recompense to, and will restore positive relations with, his family: he 'must perform against himself the act of an enemy in order to become once more his own friend and a friend of his own *philoi*'.[45] He yields to the Atreids in the sense that he pays for his disobedience and hostility towards them with his life. He exacts the vengeance on himself which they are obliged to seek from him. In short, he does their job for them. But he will use his suicide as an opportunity to curse them and wish for vengeance on them via the Erinyes (Furies). By killing himself when he did not manage actually to murder the Atreids, he is paying his debt with interest: 'Ajax's enemies are now in his debt, owing him the honour he can appropriately ask the Erinyes to exact in the form of retribution'.[46] Ajax is thus only yielding to the Atreids so that they will in turn yield to him: this is in accordance with the Anaximandrian principle of alternation and 'hostile reciprocity' which he outlines in the speech. In a world where one is in someone else's debt or wanting to exact payment from someone else, constant and unqualified friendships or enmities are impossible.

We should note here that the Greek words for 'friend' (*philos*) and 'friendship' (*philia*) seem to refer to relationships between people who are related by blood or marriage *as well as* people who are close but unrelated by kinship.[47] They also cover relationships where the bond is characterised by loyalty or duties of care as much as affection. Thus we could translate *philia* as 'kinship' or 'friendship' depending on the context. And in many cases we should take the context to indicate that

one's 'kin' and 'friends' are covered by the terms *philia*.
Capturing what it means to be a *philos* is tricky and subject to
constant debate and modification. *Philia* characterises those
who are linked by reciprocal duties of respect (*aidôs*) towards
each other: it 'clearly implies a wider notion than one purely of
sentiment'.[48]

Philia also governs hospitality and 'guest-friendship' relations (*xenia*) and is constituted by a complex set of obligations
and duties. These elements start to be configured differently
(from their expression in Homer) once a *civic* discourse
develops in Athens. The powerful ethic of 'help friends, harm
enemies' which is strong in Homer and persists in the fifth
century, was 'perhaps the most basic and generally agreed position with regard to correct behaviour in the ancient world'.[49]
But tragedy, and especially *Ajax*, seem to explore the way in
which this ethic can be subject to conflicting obligations or
imperatives, and this exploration must in part be derived from
newly constructed discourses of duty and self-positioning which
are occasioned by the rise of the democratic polis. It may be
impossible securely to determine Ajax's stance on friendship in
the deception speech. But his remarks, coupled with Odysseus'
effective deployment of 'mutability', show that the *Ajax* speaks
directly to a fundamental problem in Athenian popular
morality. 'Help friends and harm enemies' is a code which can
lead to contradictory results: Ajax's implacable hostility
towards the Atreids results in *harm* to his *philoi*. But the
compromises and qualified loyalties implied by Bias' maxim are
also problematic. For at the same time as this maxim offers a
solution to endless vendetta and hatred, it also promotes relationships which are freighted with mistrust. It can even be
deployed to excuse failures of duty and obligation between
philoi. We will see that the Bias maxim works wonders when
Odysseus puts it to work. But Ajax's more mysterious and troubling articulation of the maxim perhaps leads an audience to
see the costs of 'mutability' as well as the benefits.

Ajax moves to the last section of the deception speech by
saying 'it will turn out well' (684). Tecmessa and the Chorus
can think that this signals Ajax's resolve to live but the darker

meaning is that he will solve these problems of *philia* by killing himself. He asks Tecmessa to go inside and pray to the gods 'that what my heart desires may be accomplished right to the end' (686). Ajax's vagueness is ominous and his ambiguous language hints at a passionate desire for death.[50] And while we may think of him at last showing compassion towards Tecmessa in this speech, this final request seem heartless: 'it is a cruel command to Tecmessa to pray for his self-destruction'.[51]

Next, he tells the Chorus of sailors to go inside also (687-8). It is highly unusual for a Chorus to leave the stage in the course of a play in our extant corpus. Ajax's command shows that he intends to do something which requires his complete solitude. He also asks the sailors to tell Teucer to care for 'us' if he should come: a reference here, then, to his previous injunctions about Eurysaces' protection (562-73). But it also foreshadows Teucer's central role in securing Ajax's burial. Ajax concludes his fine speech in the language of the mysteries. But his closing remarks are also significant at a more obvious level (690-2):

> For I am going where I must journey, but you must do what I tell you, and perhaps you may soon learn that, even if I am unhappy now, I have been saved.

Of course, Tecmessa and the Chorus think that he is 'journeying' to the sea-shore. But he is actually referring to his planned journey to the underworld. By saying that he has been 'saved' he 'ends emphatically with the most striking ambiguity of all'.[52] For Ajax, death is in fact his salvation and his only means of preserving his excellence.[53]

So Ajax's speech ends with yet more ambiguity. It could be argued that his language is *so* ambiguous throughout that he utters not a single word of actual falsehood.[54] This ambiguity may be 'more important than any certainty (remote in any case) about Ajax's aims'.[55] According to Segal, the difficulty of interpreting his riddling language and securing his meanings and motivations are an important aspect of his isolation and independence as a tragic hero. The barrier between Ajax and those around him creates an 'imperfect communication' which 'fuses and confuses reality and appearance, yielding and firmness, truth and falsehood'.[56] It is only at 815-65 that he is able to bring together word and deed in a 'death speech' where medium and intention are again one.

We could also connect the pervasive ambiguities of the deception speech with the play's running theme of 'mind and madness'. The speech 'seems to set up an explanation as if it indicated the emotion, thought, reasoning, of Ajax, only to block such a move from words to mind, returning always to the fencing hesitations of language'.[57] We cannot be sure of what Ajax means, what he intends to do or what he is doing intentionally – and that is the whole point. When we see him kill himself as he curses the Atreids this only serves to problematise the relation of Ajax's words to his mind. Goldhill argues that if we try to explain the deception speech with reference to a univocal reading of Ajax's mind and intentions (as most critics do) we miss the point that its doubleness and ambiguity cannot be reduced to 'a simple singularity of intention'.[58]

But the speech's ambiguity does not exclusively convey 'uncertainty'. Rather, this doubleness may also encapsulate the hero's sophistication in deliberation. For example, Ajax has *both* a positive *and* a negative point to make about limiting the nature and extent of one's hostilities and friendships. On the plus side, such limitations protect a man from the worst effects of treachery and they also prevent him from taking his hatred to violent extremes. On the minus side, one can never fully trust one's friends, rely on their eternal and unconditional loyalty or expect comrades to treat one justly. It seems to me that Ajax's insight is not so much that 'limited' or 'qualified' relations of amity and hostility are wholly good or that they are wholly bad. Rather, he can see both sides of the coin. Perhaps he is even deliberating with himself by couching qualified friendship in terms which bring out the 'two-sidedness' of the issue.

The deliberative and rational nature of the deception speech should not be missed.[59] Ajax exhibits what modern philosophers call 'intellectual' or 'epistemic' virtue.[60] This concept has an ancient pedigree. Aristotle saw that intellectual virtues were a necessary requirement for anyone to be truly good (Aristotle

Nicomachean Ethics 1139a1-1145a11). In order to act virtuously in a moral sense, a person needs to be good at all sorts of brain work: good at deliberating over different courses of action and at seeing different viewpoints, good at overcoming biases or prejudices, good at reasoning and forming judgements, good at understanding and correctly perceiving the situation she is in and so on. These intellectual virtues or 'excellences' (*aretai*), become particularly important when agents are faced with terrible dilemmas. Greek tragedy is full of characters facing horrible decisions where all options for action seem morally reprehensible or where the attribution of justice and blame is crucial but difficult. Consequently, philosophers have seen the genre as a kind of literary exploration of how hard it is to be good.[61] Sometimes tragic characters seem to be doing well within the constraints of unavoidable ignorance and divine planning. At other times, they display defects of character, emotion and intellect which enhance their culpability or hasten their destruction.

Ajax deliberates and muses on his situation from a detached position. Of course, we have seen him being reflective and deliberative before (430-80). But unlike his 'choice of lives' speech, the deception speech figures the pros and cons of 'yielding', 'flexibility' and 'mutability' via the strategy of ambiguity – this is *not* like the deliberations of Homer's heroes. But at the same time as the speech exemplifies Ajax's attainment of a new level and mode of deliberation and intellectual virtue, it also provides a challenge to the intellectual virtues of its internal and external audiences. Tecmessa and the Chorus berate themselves for not seeing Ajax's true intentions. When Ajax's corpse is discovered, the Chorus mourn their 'delusion' (*atas*: 909): 'I, deaf to everything, ignorant in everything, paid no heed. Where, where lies the inflexible Ajax, of the ill-omened name?' (911-14). Of course, it is hard to blame Tecmessa or the Chorus for letting Ajax disappear alone. They learn of Calchas' prophecy too late and hence are not in full possession of all the relevant facts of Ajax's predicament when they are listening to the deception speech. But we have seen that the speech contains clues which the external audience may well pick up on. Thus Ajax's speech and suicide demonstrate how easy it is to misinterpret or under-interpret the evidence of our eyes and ears. It shows how difficult it is not just to hear what we want to hear. It evinces the importance and difficulty of achieving critical distance and interpretive skill in the struggle to avoid false beliefs about the world and those who inhabit it. In that sense, the deception speech paradoxically and powerfully conveys a double truth, namely the imperfection *and* importance of human under-standing.

Hope becomes despair (693-814)

As Ajax and Tecmessa go their separate ways, the Chorus step forward to sing their second *stasimon*. Because the audience must be left feeling very uneasy by the deception speech, the Chorus' cries of joy and rapture at Ajax's apparent change of heart must provoke a deep sense of tragic irony. It is especially poignant that they describe this change in terms of time's effects: 'Great time (*megas chronos*) extinguishes all things and kindles them; and I would say that nothing can be declared impossible, when beyond my hopes (*aelptôn*) Ajax has been converted from his anger against the sons of Atreus and from his mighty quarrels' (714-18). This language directly echoes that of Ajax (646-8). But at the same time as such echoing underlines the fact that they have swallowed Ajax's surface meanings, our worry that he will kill himself means that they are more right than they realise when they predict an end to Ajax's dispute with the Atreids.

The messenger's arrival quickly curtails the Chorus's mood of elation. His description of the hostile reception which Teucer has received on returning to the Greek camp is disturbing. Such is the army's anger and suspicion towards Ajax that they are threatening the 'madman' with death. Teucer and his assailants unsheathed their swords and the quarrel only ceased through 'old men's reconciling words' (732). Here we are reminded of the quarrel between Agamemnon and Achilles in *Iliad* 1 and the role Nestor plays in mediating it. But the messenger's vivid picture also gives us a sense of the very real hostility and threats which Teucer will face in defending his brother.

When he learns that Ajax has already left his tent, the messenger laments that he has arrived too late (737-8). Indeed the entire scene in which the messenger explains why it was imperative for Ajax to be accompanied and kept indoors develops a 'too late' motif where all those who have a stake in keeping the hero alive will be frustrated by time. However, the fact that the hero and Chorus have both marked time's power to reveal unexpected outcomes might lead an audience to hope that Ajax may yet be saved. And Calchas himself has held out the hope that 'perhaps we might turn out to be his saviours with the help of a god' (779-80).

The messenger gives a long account of Calchas' explanation of the reasons for Ajax's madness (748-83). This report draws on Calchas' Homeric role as a prophet who explains the gods' role in shaping the fate of the Greeks' campaign at Troy. It has been a focus for critical debate over the extent and nature of Ajax's responsibility for his own tragedy, not to mention his specific brand of heroic extremism and the question of whether or not he is being punished for being 'hubristic' towards Athena. I will defer full discussion of these issues until my final chapter. For now, it is important to highlight Calchas' very specific gloss on the causes of Athena's 'ruthless fury' against Ajax (777).

First, before he even arrives in Troy there is Ajax's boastful reply to his father that 'together with the gods even the non-entity could achieve victory, but *I* trust that even without them I shall win glory (*kleos*)' (767-9). This boast rebuts Telamon's advice that he must wish for his victories to be divinely aided. But the messenger and Calchas also emphasise the fact that this attitude is derived from *intellectual* failings: his rejection of the divine is 'stupid', 'lacking in understanding' and 'thoughtlessly' conceived (758, 763, 766). Secondly, this boast and Ajax's later verbal rejection of Athena's help during battle are described as 'non-human' thinking and taboo. Calchas has explained that 'it is only for today that the wrath of Athena still drives him' (756-7). But this is because 'it is bodies grown too great and stupid' that fall at the hands of the gods, and they do so 'whenever a man is born with a human nature (*anthrôpou phusin*), but does not think in accordance with his human status' (758-62).

Calchas' privileged status as a prophet gives the messenger's report divine authority and I can see no reason for discounting its importance as an explanation for Ajax's predicament.[62] Crucially, Ajax displays a lack of understanding and a character which trangresses his 'nature' as a human. As a human, Ajax should realise that he needs, and must embrace, divine aid and approval. For all the critics' claims that this is 'typical' behaviour for a Sophoclean hero, Ajax's extreme arrogance taints his 'greatness' with stupidity and impiety. And the revelation that Ajax's downfall is partly derived from his intellectual failings underscores the significance of his deception speech and final death speech as an example of newly-acquired intellectual virtue: Ajax *does* finally consider yielding to the gods and calls on the help of Zeus, Hermes and (more chillingly) the non-Olympian vengeance-godesses, the Furies (666, 824-44). Calchas' words suggest that Ajax has been exhibiting failings of character and understanding ever since he set sail for Troy.

When the messenger finishes his devastating news, Tecmessa enters to learn the truth of the situation (787-802). Teucer is on his way to help prevent disaster but she quickly organises a search for the hero and will join in it herself (803-12). It is a mark of her generous character that she still wishes to save Ajax even though she feels rejected by him.

Curse and self-slaughter (815-977)

Tecmessa, the messenger and the Chorus exit to search for Ajax. It is unusual for the Chorus to depart in the middle of a play like this, and their later re-entrance indicates that they divide in two to take two different exits. Ajax's entrance at 815 indicates a scene change. We are now in a lonely spot which, in line with Ajax's comments at 654-9, we may imagine is close to the seashore.[63]

Ajax first tells us that 'the killer (*sphageus*) stands where, if one has the leisure for calculation, it might cut most effectively' (815-6). He is personifying the sword as a murderer. He says that it comes from Hector, the 'most loathed' of his guest-friends – here we have a continuation of Ajax's heroic recharacterisation of the sword and its paradoxical qualities of friendship and hostility. But *sphageus* can also denote the agent of a ritual sacrificial killing. This imagery (also found at 658-9) answers Ajax's perverted 'sacrifice' of the army's beasts: 'in a sense the chorus' image at 711-713 is correct ... he is making peace with the gods and the cosmic order but on his own terms. His is a private sacrifice, the celebrant fused with the victim; the rest of the community, the normal beneficiary of such a sacrifice, is excluded.'[64]

Ajax describes how he has fixed the newly-sharpened sword in the ground, 'hoping that it will be very kind to me and grant me a speedy death' (821). He prays that Zeus may send Teucer a message so that his brother will find his body before his enemies cast it out as prey for dogs and birds (824-30). Here we have some clear preparation for the imminent quarrel over whether or not Ajax's body can be buried. He also prays that Hermes may put him swiftly to sleep when he has leapt on the sword and torn his side with it (834).

Ajax is describing in uncomfortable detail exactly how he will kill himself. He is one of only three males in tragedy to commit suicide – self-caused death is usually the preserve of heroines. Belfiore argues persuasively that Ajax's suicide is different from that of Menoikeus in Euripides' *Phoenician Women* and Haimon in Sophocles' *Antigone*.[65] The former kills himself in a heroic fashion to save his polis in war. The latter kills himself after a failed attempt to kill his father (Creon) and it looks very much like a shameful vengeance suicide in which he uses his own death as a curse and cause of pollution. Loraux notes that the Greek language lacks a special word for suicide, resorting instead to the same words (*autophonos* and *autocheir*) as are used for the murder of parents – 'the ultimate ignominy'.[66] Examples of suicide in the historical accounts of Herodotus and Xenophon indicate that self-caused death can be admired in certain circumstances.[67] But if it is often the means by which warriors respond to shame and dishonour, it is not therefore to be regarded as noble. Euripides' Heracles kills his family in a fit of madness but he finally rejects suicide because it is a form of cowardice (*Heracles Furens* 1348). Ajax does not have the options of purification and a new life which Theseus offers to Heracles. Perhaps his circumstances fit more closely with Plato's belief that suicide can be excused if it relieves 'the intolerable pain of misfortune from which there is no way out' (*Laws* 9.873c5-6). But one cannot get away from the fact that suicide or even seeking death too openly in battle are often figured as unmanly or reprehensible in our classical sources.[68] At the same time, however, we should not forget that Homer's Odysseus and Achilles both contemplate suicide when they are at their lowest ebb, with the latter having to be restrained so that he will not cut his own throat.[69] Although it is highly problematic, self-caused death is very much part of the archaic and classical grammar of military identity and psychology.

Ajax clearly thinks that suicide *is* a noble option (479-80). As for 'manliness', Loraux has shown how Ajax's particular mode of suicide is markedly different from the methods of suicide adopted or contemplated by tragic heroines. He uses the sword rather than a rope or noose, and he will pierce his side (*pleuran*) – these are paradigms of the *manly* suicide.[70] The sword is 'firm-standing' (*hestêken*) – a description which could be used of a hoplite standing upright at his post. But Loraux also argues that the manner of Ajax's suicide is not *completely* manly. His swift 'leap' (*pêdêma*) onto the blade invokes the same vocabulary used of feminine tragic suicides by hanging or jumping onto a pyre.

We should perhaps set Ajax's own self-representation of his suicide as a noble death dealt by an enemy 'killer' next to contextual hints that it is a 'a poor imitation of a warrior's noble death'.[71] But it would be unwise to judge Ajax's suicide only in terms of contextual material or other tragic suicides. Ajax's very particular circumstances and reasons for such extreme action are underlined by his vehement curse on the Atreids. He calls on the Furies who facilitate vengeance to 'learn how in my wretchedness I am being destroyed by the sons of Atreus' (837-8). With startling ferocity he asks the Furies to 'devour them' and 'spare not the whole body of the army' (844). Ajax does not simply see himself as choosing a noble way out – his enemies are *causing* his destruction and he demands retribution as a result.

Burnett has recently argued that Ajax's vengeful curse is 'as anomalous and almost as sensational as is the staged suicide'.[72] The form of Ajax's curse is unique for its closeness to the cursing formulae found in real magical papyri – it was felt to be dangerous even to imitate these formulae. The Furies will be attracted by the blood and gore which (we are later told) gushes from his nose and huge wound (918-19, 1411-12). Thus the suicide and the curse are one and the same thing in terms of dramatic effect and intention. They work together to 'show Ajax's characteristic arrogance as it finally identifies itself with forces more than human'.[73] The Furies are a new set of divine allies who replace Athena. Ironically for a man who previously rejected divine aid, argues Burnett, he 'hands his rage and his revenge over to the crude justice of bloodsucking demons' who will strike the Greek army at their own discretion. The curse is also significant because Sophocles has ensured that it is performed in secret – only the audience knows about it. Even though Odysseus has seen the raving vengeful Ajax and the results of his secret mission at the beginning of the play, he does not know that the 'same man did the same work over again with resolve and control, his action fully his own. Only they [the audience] recognise the self-drawn black blood as an active force that engages the daimonic world'.[74] We may question Burnett's certainty that Ajax's action is 'fully his own' here. But she is right to insist that the curse betokens Ajax's very particular method of dying with honour – the curse/suicide combination enables him to enact vengeance from beyond the grave.

We may find it hard to square this curse with Ajax's earlier claim to have learned *sôphrosunê*. And it is significant that he enlists the aid of non-Olympian divinities who represent violent vendetta. But the remainder of his speech is filled with calm and pathos as he asks the sun to report his death to his parents, imagines his mother's laments and says farewell to Salamis, Athens and the Trojan plains (845-65). After Ajax has leapt on his sword, the Chorus enter and bemoan the fact that that they cannot find their leader (866-90). It is Tecmessa who discovers the body, unseen by the Chorus (891). She and the Chorus share in lamenting Ajax's death and fearing for their future now that they are exposed to their enemies. Tecmessa hopes that Teucer will arrive soon so that the body can be buried. But she also imagines the laughter and mockery of Ajax's enemies and Odysseus' insults in particular. She predicts that the loss of Ajax's martial prowess will turn that laughter to sorrow: 'people of poor judgement do not realise the advantages they have in their hands until they are thrown away' (964-5). In this way, Tecmessa uses her last words in the tragedy to convey her own intellect and the negative consequences of inadequate understanding on the part of others. She also builds suspense and concern over how Ajax's body is to be treated and sets the audience up for the arguments and surprises of the final scenes. She will be proved wrong about Odysseus – his measured appreciation of Ajax's positive qualities will mirror her own. Nevertheless, her grief, wisdom and loyalty in this scene evince a form of 'nobility' which makes it hard for us to be certain that Ajax has really performed a 'noble' act.

Ajax's suicide presents a very difficult problem of staging. As Garvie puts it, 'in no other surviving tragedy does violent death take place before the eyes of the audience, and it is not certain that it does so here'.[75] There are three main reasons for doubting that Ajax leaps onto his sword in full view of the audience. First, it would be technically difficult to stage the business of falling on a blade. Secondly, the 'three-actor rule' means that the actor who plays Ajax must soon play Teucer and so cannot remain on stage as a lifeless corpse until the end of the play. Thirdly, the Chorus indicates that Tecmessa finds the corpse just out of sight of the audience (892). And yet, Ajax's shrouded dead body is visible from 992 onwards or possibly earlier. This means either that a fourth actor played Teucer – a very unlikely solution – or that the actor playing Ajax is somehow substituted with a dummy or an 'extra'.

One way of overcoming these problems is to have Ajax fall behind a screen which has been brought on-stage as the hero enters at 815. This means that the sword fixed in the ground is never visible to the audience and they infer its position and existence from Ajax's vivid descriptions of it in his death speech. But this solution soon runs into problems because it requires Tecmessa to be behind the screen when she finds the body (891) and then to emerge from it at 894, leaving the corpse improbably unattended.

Garvie surmises that a screen could come on at 915 when Tecmessa says that she will cover the corpse with a shroud.[76] This way, Ajax falls on his sword in full view of the audience with the stunt being facilitated by a retractable blade. We know such 'stage swords' were used in later periods.[77] Then, while Tecmessa and Ajax are hidden by the screen, the actor walks off unseen via the central door in the *skênê* and is substituted by a dummy corpse or an extra playing dead. The rest of Tecmessa's exchange with the Chorus is conducted from behind the screen (915-73). When Teucer arrives, his words ('Oh beloved eye of my brother') do not mean that he can see the body (977). This reference to his brother's eye or face may simply be a metaphor, which can be glossed as 'brotherly source of light to me'. Garvie argues that it is only at 992 that the shrouded corpse becomes visible to Teucer – his cry there is a reaction to the removal of the screen – and only at 1004 is the shroud removed to reveal Ajax's face.

This is a neat solution to the whole problem. But Garvie's screen seems rather clumsy and Teucer's cry at 977 may not be metaphorical. Other critics have been uneasy with the technicalities of an on-stage suicide and have suggested use of the *ekkuklêma* as a means of substituting an actor for a dummy.[78] The main objection to using the *ekkuklêma* for the suicide is that all the evidence points to its exclusive deployment for the revelation or discovery of internal scenes.[79] Heath stages the scene on the basis of simplicity and the absence of any clues in the text for elaborate props, scenery or machinery: Ajax enters at 815 to describe what he has just done off-stage, namely fix the sword in the ground. At the end of the death speech, he exits via the central door to kill himself off-stage. A body is then carried on by stage hands.[80] But Heath concedes that there is just no way of knowing for sure how the scene was managed and cites a convention from Chinese theatre to show how worthless our own intuitions about staging might be: 'if an execution is to be enacted, a packet encased in red silk signifies the severed head; the man executed runs off stage, and an assistant displays the packet to the audience'.[81]

If we cannot be sure of exactly how the suicide was staged, we can at least appreciate its originality for the extant tragic corpus and its thematic impact. Ajax kills himself violently and in total isolation. No one but the audience hears his curse on the Atreids. And his body remains on stage as a focal point for the lamentation and quarrelling which is played out in the rest of the tragedy.

6

The Quarrel

Relevance, unity and dramatic effect

The concluding debate-scenes of the play have been called drawn-out, anticlimactic and undramatic – *untragic* even. Some have also argued that the post-death quarrel is irrelevant to, or lacks unity with, the main thrust of the play and its focus on Ajax's downfall.

An ancient scholiast started the assault on the dramatic effectiveness of these scenes: 'this kind of quibbling is inappropriate to tragedy. After the death of Ajax, Sophocles, wishing to stretch the play out, grew cold and undid its tragic pathos' (scholion on 1123). This view (often echoed by modern critics) relies on an anachronistic aesthetic in which earthy personal invective is (wrongly) seen to be incompatible with an Homeric and fifth-century 'heroic' ethos. Nor does it take into account the powerful 'entertainment value' offered by the performance of these angry scenes. Contrast the reaction of the scholar Jebb when he saw *Ajax* put on as the first ever Cambridge Greek Play in 1882: 'the *Ajax* as a whole is a thoroughly effective play for the stage ... its power of holding an audience is not diminished by the death of the hero at a comparatively early moment in the action'.[1] If Jebb's Cambridge liked the final scenes, Sophocles' Athens would have loved them because they spoke so directly to its culture of performance and rhetorical debate. This is not to say that the 'double debate-scene' structure of the final quarrel is a standard one. The stalemate between Teucer and the Atreids is underscored by its unusual length. One effect of this elongation is to showcase Odysseus by displaying the need for his skill at negotiating.

The second charge of disunity and irrelevance has few

supporters these days: Sophocles clearly prepares us for 'unfinished business' and a crisis over Ajax's burial long before the hero's suicide. But there are more pertinent differences of opinion about the dramatic tone and thematic function of the debate-scenes and final resolution. Here is an example of the most common reading:

> The play's finale pays a measure of respect to Ajax's greatness, shows the smallness of the post-heroic world which is left after his passing, exalts the humanity of Odysseus in contrast to both the stark individualism of Ajax and the pettiness of the Atreids, and insures Ajax's hero-cult through proper burial
>
> Holt, 'Debate Scenes', pp. 281-2

This formulation has much to recommend it – the phrase 'a measure of respect' leaves room for the point that Ajax's negative qualities and actions are not completely whitewashed by his or anybody else's rhetoric. And it is true that the final scenes shift us much closer to the fifth-century agora in order to explore tensions between fifth-century and Homeric values. But the world of the final scenes is not as 'small', 'petty' or as 'post-heroic' as is often supposed. Nor is it only Ajax and Odysseus whose differing styles of heroism are lauded in this world. A key figure in this chapter's adjustment to the common reading is Teucer: his successful vitriol and earthy commitment to his brother have been missed, misunderstood or unfairly downgraded by critics.[2] Teucer is not just some mediocre substitute for Ajax.[3] As for Menelaus and Agamemnon, they may be despicable villains who are 'far removed from their Homeric counterparts',[4] but, as we will see, they also they raise pertinent objections to Ajax's brand of self-assertion from the vantage point of the post-Homeric polis-dweller.

Teucer and Menelaus (974-1072)

Teucer's arrival at the beginning of the fourth episode has been much-anticipated by characters and Chorus – it is something of a dramatic climax. Teucer had acted promptly to convey the message that Ajax should not leave his tent. His appearance thus emphasises the play's motifs of divine control and 'too-lateness'. Indeed, as the Chorus help him to come to terms with the spectacle of his brother's corpse, Teucer cries: 'Oh over-hasty misfortune' (982). Ajax's fate has been swiftly sealed despite his brother's best efforts – there is a strong suggestion here that the wrath of Athena is ineluctable. But Teucer's arrival also brings other themes of the play into a new and final phase. While the last five hundred lines do underline Ajax's greatness by contrasting his life with the attitudes of his detractors, the quarrelling and eventual accommodation also explore shortcomings in, and alternatives to, Ajax's ethos and brand of masculinity.

Issues of identity and status surround Teucer. He and Ajax do not have the same mother – Teucer is the bastard progeny of Telamon and his Trojan (and thus barbarian) spear-bride, Hesione (sister of king Priam). He is an ethnic hybrid who wields a bow.[5] His identity thus falls well short of the classical civic ideal of the all-Greek hoplite warrior, and the Atreids' snobbery will bring this out.[6] The play has already asked what would constitute action appropriate to Ajax's noble birth (*eugeneia*) and identity as a 'big' Greek spear-man. Teucer's lower status and his clash with the chauvinistic Atreids allows Sophocles to meditate further on the relationship between reputation, status, identity and action. This meditation is part of the play's wider examination of the clash between traditional notions of 'nobility' and newer, more egalitarian definitions which were prompted by (though not necessarily embedded in) Athenian democracy. But Teucer is not, in any straightforward sense, Sophocles' cipher for the 'ordinary' Athenian citizen. For, as we will see, his identity is problematic in specifically *Athenian* terms.

Homer's Ajax protected Teucer (*Iliad* 8.266-72). Now the situation is reversed: Teucer has to take on the role of a Homeric hero protecting the corpse of a comrade. Will he defend Eurysaces and secure Ajax's burial as the hero had requested? He meets the sight of Tecmessa and the Chorus standing over Ajax's body with a combination of questions and cries of lamentation (974-84, 992-1027). His '*Iô moi moi*' echoes the cries of Tecmessa (891, 937). It also echoes Ajax in his struggle to comprehend his situation (333, 336). Teucer's closeness to Ajax and Tecmessa is thus demonstrated through a shared language of anguish and mourning. But we should also remember that Ajax cried out for his brother in vain (343-4). Teucer feels that he did nothing to help Ajax in his hour of need (1007). His tenacity must be understood in the light of this worry.

Teucer intensifies the dramatic focus on the corpse because he addresses it directly – as if his brother were still alive (992-1005). His closeness to Ajax may have been further emphasised if, as seems likely, it was the same actor who played both brothers.[7] Such a distribution of parts would also highlight Teucer's role as Ajax's living representative and thus lend support to a view that the bowman has a greatness of his own.

Despite his grief, Teucer quickly dispatches the Chorus and Tecmessa to bring Eurysaces to him. He worries that the Atreids may snatch the boy away 'like the whelp of a bereaved lioness' (986-7; compare Homer *Iliad* 18.318-23).[8] This Homeric-style simile compares Tecmessa to a (fierce) lioness and suggests that Ajax's son has the qualities of his father (the implied lion). But the Homeric register is also an act of self-assertion: Teucer needs to project heroic stature in order to face enemies who will try to belittle him in every way. It is notable that Teucer moves to bring Eurysaces into his protection immediately and before any prompting from the Chorus – they merely confirm that Teucer is acting as Ajax had enjoined (990-1). Sophocles seems to be stressing that Teucer has it in his *nature* to do the right thing by Ajax – he does not need to be told – and it is his very nature (*phusis*) which Agamemnon will soon impugn as barbarous, ignoble and slavish (1259-63). When they see Menelaus approaching, the Chorus do have to prompt Teucer to start thinking about how Ajax is to be buried (1040-3). But there is no suggestion that Teucer needs persuading of the need to bury his brother. He is not a male Antigone – he is less isolated for a start – but his brave and decisive attitude is closer to hers than that of Sophoclean siblings like Ismene and Chrysothemis, characters who are too frightened to risk their lives in defence of dead relatives.

Interestingly, Teucer is more afraid of his father (Telamon) than he is of the Atreids. In this, and several other respects, Teucer's first long speech echoes both the form and content of Ajax's deliberations. But where Ajax expects a charge of cowardice and disgrace, Teucer fears a whole range of paranoid insults and accusations from his father when he finds out that Ajax is dead: 'the bastard born of the enemy's spear, the man who betrayed you, dearest Ajax, by cowardice and unmanliness (*kakandriai*), or deceit, so that I might administer your power and house when you are dead!' (1013-16). Teucer assumes that he will have a worse time of it because he is illegitimate: he expects to be exiled by bad-tempered old Telamon and imagines himself reduced to the status of a slave as a result (1019-20). According to tradition, Teucer's fears were realised: having been banished by Telamon he founded Salamis in Cyprus.[9] This banishment probably formed the subject of the *Teucer*, a Sophoclean tragedy which, apart from a few tantalising lines, is lost. Perhaps our play begins a process of positive representation which the *Teucer* completed, namely the celebration of Ajax's brother as a worthy and manly founder of a second Salamis.[10] But the primary point about Teucer's concerns is they that underline the extent to which Ajax's suicide is likely to turn his brother's life upside down. It is to Ajax's discredit that he did not even consider such an outcome in his deliberations.

Teucer's fear of enslavement echoes both Tecmessa's fears and the fate which she and Teucer's mother have already endured. Teucer's situation also mirrors the fate which threatens Eurysaces – they are both the bastard-children of spear-captives. These parallel fates are important because they declare that 'free birth and slavery are gifts of fortune and not legitimate criteria of human worth'.[11] This is a crucial point in the debate-scenes that follow.

Like Ajax, Teucer neither can face staying in Troy surrounded by hostility, nor can he go home (1019-23; 458-65).

And he echoes his brother's exasperated paralysis: 'Alas, what shall I do?' (1024; 457). Why does Sophocles stress these similarities of outlook and attitude between Teucer and Ajax at this point? For one thing, we see that Ajax's sense of shame and failure is not entirely self-generated: Telamon is a judgmental presence for *both* brothers. We have already noted this tragedy's pervasive interest in the relationship between fathers and sons and Athenian society's valorisation of fatherly authority. Teucer is adding to this play's implicit critique of the way in which a father's character and expectations can damage and depress his offspring.

Teucer may echo his brother's fears but he is an improvement on him in certain respects. For a start, 'Ajax bequeaths to his brother the crisis that he himself died rather than face'.[12] Even if we think that Ajax has made provision for his *philoi*, he still leaves them all in a difficult predicament. Saddled with great responsibility, Teucer chooses to stand by his *philoi*: Ajax, Tecmessa and Eurysaces will all benefit from his decision to risk his own life by facing the Atreids. To be sure, Ajax's decision to kill himself is an 'exemplary gesture' but Teucer's decision to stay alive and argue tenaciously with Ajax's enemies is admirable.

Teucer concludes his long speech by reflecting on the way in which the fates of Ajax and Hector are intertwined (1028-30). Hector's sword is a 'killer' (1026). And the gift which Ajax gave (a war belt) was used to strap Hector to Achilles' chariot. Achilles then dragged (and mangled) his body until he 'gasped out his life' (1031).[13] Teucer is continuing Ajax's 'heroic' recharacterisation of the sword. Like Tecmessa and the Chorus, Teucer senses that the gods are behind everything (1034-7). But his choice of gods and words has real bite – the sword is like an agent of Hector's vengeance: hence the 'Fury' made it. And Hades is the *agrios demiourgos* of the belt: this means 'savage craftsman', but the word for 'craftsman' has the more literal sense of 'he who works for the people' – a sardonic soubriquet for the god of death. Not for the last time, Teucer displays a witty facility with words and ideas.[14]

Menelaus' entry heralds the second formal debate-scene

(*agôn*) of the play.[15] This conventional feature of Greek tragedy (and comedy) reflects the Athenians' fondness for debate and verbal contest, not to mention the fact that their legal and political system relied completely on rhetorical contests between individual speakers before mass audiences who sat in judgement and deliberation. It is usually the case that the long speeches in tragic *agônes* share strategies and language with surviving examples of real Athenian law-court rhetoric and political oratory, not to mention the display speeches and rhetorical theories of fifth-century sophists. Often, the points at issue in an *agôn* are not only relevant to the tragedy's characters – they are rendered in such a way that they seem to speak directly to (what we can guess were) the concerns of the Athenian audience.[16] The formal debate-scenes at the end of our play are no exception to this.

Menelaus is immediately provocative: Teucer must not arrange burial for Ajax's corpse (1047-8). The bowman asks him why. Because he and Agamemnon have decided on it, says the king. Here is the unattractive rigidity and intransigence which he and his brother will maintain throughout – although we should remember that Ajax himself has displayed these traits. Menelaus then goes into a long rhetorical explanation for the decision. First, he indicts Ajax for being a 'worse enemy' than the Trojans when he should have been an ally (1052-4). This is a fair point but exaggeration is already creeping in: Menelaus says that Ajax 'plotted murder against the whole army' (1055). We know that Ajax only intended to kill the leaders.[17] Because of his attempted crime, Ajax must remain unburied (1064-5). Menelaus regards this prohibition on burial as a belated means of exerting power and control over a man who would never listen to or obey Menelaus when he was alive (1066-70).

This stance is repulsive and vindictive. From a fifth-century Greek perspective, it is fundamentally hubristic and impious to deny Ajax some form of burial.[18] But we can imagine Ajax being a difficult comrade – Menelaus' complaints fit the image of Ajax not listening to advice in the Messenger's report of Calchas' words.[19] Notwithstanding Teucer's (and most critics') refusal to accept that Menelaus has any authority over Ajax, the Spartan

king has a point about the need for fear, discipline and lawful-
ness: an army cannot be controlled if soldiers do not obey
orders. Fear (*phobos / deos*) and shame (*aidôs*) help to maintain
that discipline. Similarly, a polis cannot function lawfully
without its citizens being subject to fear of punishment (1073-
6). But we must wince at Menelaus' outrageous and arrogant
assumption that Ajax is a 'commoner' (*dêmotên*) who is bad for
not obeying his 'superiors' (1071-2). This cannot have found
favour with an Athenian audience – not just because of its snobbery but because of its lack of 'fit' with Ajax's aristocratic
grandeur and Athenian associations: 'as if Ajax were some
recalcitrant Thersites!' cries one outraged critic.[20]

Anti-Spartan propaganda?

Menelaus' vileness has a deliciously transgressive quality which
the audience must have enjoyed hating. Both he and
Agamemnon are almost pantomimic in their more villainous
moments. This characterisation partly stems from the play's
historical context and partisan political ideology. *Ajax* was
probably written at a time when Athens was either at, or on the
brink of, war with Sparta. Where Athens was a democratic
polis, Sparta's constitution gave power to a narrow oligarchy
headed by two soldier-kings. Athenian texts of the fifth and
fourth centuries, of all genres, including drama, develop a
variety of assaults on Sparta's national character, constitution
and customs. The unflattering depiction of Spartans (even
'mythical' ones like Menelaus) afforded Athenians a means of
defining and exalting their own identity.[21] Some would like to
think that Sophocles rose above the sordid machinery of politics
and ideology.[22] But for those of us who believe that ideology is a
fine and an unavoidable ingredient of great literature (and the
Great Dionysia), Menelaus' contemporary colours are important. It has even been argued that Sophocles consolidates his
defence of Ajax by 'tapping [the] enormous reservoir of anti-
Spartan hostility in his audience'.[23]

Does the topicality serve only to deepen the audience's
hostility to Menelaus? Teucer's long reply to Menelaus certainly

stresses his status as a *Spartan* ruler (1102). And we can imagine Athenians becoming very partisan when Teucer attacks his arrogations of authority over others (1102-8). He says: 'You came here as ruler over Sparta, not as *our* commander'. The Athenian audience would have identified themselves with the 'our' here, perhaps even raising a 'patriotic cheer'.[24]

But Menelaus' authoritarianism should be viewed through a double lens. On the one hand, yes, he does seem to bring a tyrannical, fifth-century and Spartan standard of hierarchy and discipline into play.[25] His stress on *fear* as an important element of politico-military discipline chimes with Plutarch's observation that (at least in the third century BC) the Spartan Ephors had a shrine to Fear near their dining hall because they believed that their 'political system was especially kept intact by fear' (*Cleomenes* 9). On the other hand, there is nothing in what Menelaus says about the need for discipline which could not have been uttered by an *Athenian* general or demagogue. For example, the Thucydidean Pericles says that all Athenians 'are prevented from doing wrong by fear of the authorities and the laws' (2.37.3).[26] In Aeschylus' *Eumenides*, the patron goddess of Athens herself makes the point that fear is necessary in a city (696-9). Menelaus' strictures are even consonant with the oath sworn by every Athenian as they attained their status as citizen-hoplites.[27]

The fact that Menelaus says things which are as much Athenian as they are Spartan may not make much difference to his image. Menelaus still revolts us because of his *application* of these principles of discipline to the particular case of Ajax and his refusal to grant a burial. His corrupt definition of *sôphrosunê* amounts to the instruction, 'always obey me'. But Menelaus' polis-based rhetoric does still have unsettling resonances for watching Athenians. This rhetoric echoes certain pronouncements made by Creon in Sophocles' *Antigone*.[28] Creon starts this play sounding like a democratic-style general who serves his polis and listens to advice. But he quickly becomes an unheeding and hubristic tyrant. This change exemplifies the ease with which a democratic polis can become a tyrannical one.[29] Menelaus' authoritarianism similarly invites an audience to think carefully about rights, responsibilities and the limits of authority in their own polis. Perhaps they leave the theatre of Dionysus making a mental note not to let their generals and demagogues smuggle in an oppressive oligarchy under the cover of civic doctrines. But Menelaus also makes the Athenian citizen-soldier think about his own responsibilities. In speaking as if Ajax were a hoplite under his direct command, Menelaus reminds all polis-dwellers that they cannot do whatever they like. He explicitly says 'let us not think that if we do what pleases us we shall not in turn pay a penalty that will cause us pain' (1085-6: note the generalising 'us' and 'we').

Ajax tried to kill the people who had (perhaps unfairly) dishonoured him. A contemporary audience would feel for Ajax's *atimia* (dishonour) deeply. But if you avenged *atimia* with an extra-judicial killing in fifth-century Athens or Sparta, then you would expect punishment sanctioned by state authority. And this is just one of the ways in which the 'anachronistic' fifth-century flavour of the play's closing debate scenes nuance and develop the significance of Ajax's tragedy. Menelaus makes us view Ajax under the less glamorous lights of the 'modern' polis – he has attempted extra-judicial killing because of a grievance. However much we feel sympathy for Ajax, his style of masculinity clashes with the demands of civic order. The audience can boo Menelaus because he is a Spartan bully-boy but he reminds them that they are polis-dwellers, not heroic outlaws.

A verbal beating (1087-162)

Menelaus ends his long speech by openly accusing Ajax of religious and social outrage (*hubris*): 'These things go in alternation. This man was formerly full of hot-tempered *hubris*, but now it is my turn to be proud. And so I order you ... not to bury this man ...' (1087-9). The literal translation of 'my turn to be proud' is 'my turn to think big'. In his own mind, Menelaus clearly distinguishes 'thinking big' from *hubris*. But his phrasing clumsily invites the view that he will become hubristic himself. Not for the last time, Menelaus' words rebound on him. Furthermore, his planned abuse of a former comrade's dead body indicates that 'thinking big' can amount to *hubris*. The Chorus (showing their more intelligent and confident side) quickly point this out: 'do not become a *hubristês* yourself at the expense of the dead' (1092).[30]

We will see in the next chapter that Menelaus' attributions of *hubris* to Ajax are not necessarily or entirely unfair. But, in contrast to Ajax's 'principle of alternation' in the deception-speech, Menelaus' version is debased: act hubristically towards those who have so behaved towards you. And his authoritarian view of *sôphrosunê* makes anyone who disobeys him a *hubristês*. In this respect he sounds like Athena (131-2). The same actor probably played both roles.

I have already conveyed the main thrust of Teucer's long reply to Menelaus: the Spartan had no authority over Ajax and so cannot prohibit the burial. He also impugns the relationship between Menelaus' words and his status: 'Men, I should never again be surprised at a man who is born a nobody (*mêden*) and then goes wrong, when those who seem to be born noble (*eugeneis*) speak words that are so wrong' (1093-6). He then implies that Menelaus himself is actually a 'nobody' (1114). He will not pay any attention to Menelaus' 'empty noise' (*psophou*) so long as he is the kind of man he is (1116-17). Talk of 'nobodies' was a mark of Ajax's arrogance (767). But where Ajax thought you were a 'nobody' if you fought with divine aid, Teucer's insult seems better targeted. As Tecmessa had done with Ajax himself, Teucer questions a 'big' man's assumption that his noble birth must automatically render his arguments and decisions noble. By redescribing Menelaus' rhetoric as mere noise, he completes the point (and the insult): this king is neither big nor small: he is a nobody saying nothing. No wonder the Chorus caution Teucer: 'harsh words sting even if they are more than just' (1118-19). Teucer's language is indeed extraordinarily aggressive, but he is initiating a critique of claims to 'nobility' which will culminate in his treatment of Agamemnon.

Teucer has his brother's 'harshness' but is 'harsh' with foes rather than *philoi*. And where Tecmessa discussed *eugeneia* in mollifying tones, Teucer harnesses the concept as a weapon in

114

a war of words. In a pre-emptive strike, Teucer resorts to status-related abuse before the Spartan can. But Menelaus' prejudices are easily flushed out: 'The archer apparently has no small thoughts' (1120). In the ensuing exchange of single lines of dialogue (*stichomythia*), the two men bandy insults, boasts and counter-assertions like warriors trading blows (1120-41). Teucer asserts his right to 'think big' (*mega phronein*) when he has 'justice' on his side (1120): we are meant to think of this big thought and talk as the appropriate weapon for fighting Menelaus' *hubristic* 'thinking big'. Teucer mockingly and playfully echoes Menelaus' vocabulary in order to trump each new argument or insult.[31] Menelaus does some echoing too – his responses to Teucer are weak in terms of content but they do not completely lack flair and style.[32] The quick-fire *stichomythia* is followed by two pairs of near-symmetrical short speeches, the first pair consisting of a fable-cum-riddle (*ainos* or *ainigma*) from Menelaus which is mockingly undercut by a pseudo-fable from Teucer. This is Menelaus' fable (1142-9):

> I once saw a man with ready tongue
> Urging some seamen to sail in a storm.
> But in the thick of it, you could not hear
> A sound from him, as he hid underneath
> His cloak, letting the crew walk over him at will.
> So too with your loud mouth: a mighty (*megas*) storm
> Blowing up from some tiny (*smikrou*) cloud
> Will quickly put an end to all your shouting.

Menelaus is expanding on his original theme at 1120-4 that Teucer is thinking and talking big even though he is not a big man. He is also improvising on his earlier point that even a man with a big body can fall as a result of a small misfortune (1077-8). He has attacked Teucer for being a bowman and not a hoplite, but Teucer proudly dismissed that snobbish insult; archery is not vulgar, and even if he were fully armed like a hoplite, Menelaus would be no match for the lightly-armed Teucer (1121, 1123).[33] So Menelaus tries a 'ship allegory' instead – a man can have a bold tongue and raging mouth, but when a storm comes he'll cower under a cloak being trampled by his crew.[34] Note the language of bigness and smallness again with reference to the storm and the cloud which engenders it.

Menelaus' allegory works against him in a way which we are meant to pick up on as *unintended by him* but significant for the play's thematics. As with Ajax's deception speech and Odysseus' final rhetoric of reconciliation, he articulates an idea of alternation and change: in this case, a big thing can come from something small. Without realising it, Menelaus counters his own earlier implication that the distinction between 'big' and 'small' is permanently marked out by birth and military status – because here we have a more cosmic observation on the possibility of change and transformation between bigness and smallness. This is an observation which fits with Teucer's earlier implication that Menelaus has *changed* into a 'nobody' because of what he says. It also chimes with a key notion of change that Ajax had articulated and which Odysseus will use on Agamemnon, namely that friends can become enemies and vice versa. Menelaus has unwittingly given us an image of 'mutability' which counters his own prejudices about what counts as normative masculinity. And his misapprehension is affirmed as we see the 'small' Teucer becoming a 'big' man, through this verbal duel and before our very eyes. The bowman does not just talk above his weight – he *becomes* weighty through his way with words.

But Menelaus' *intended* meaning is clear enough – so obvious, in fact, that Teucer chooses an allegorical rejoinder which is not really an allegory at all, but a mockingly transparent parody of Menelaus' unsophisticated riddle (1150-8). In this parody he makes the serious point that Menelaus' intended bad treatment of Ajax's body is *hubris* and will rebound on him. He trumps the Spartan again by wittily out-improvising him: he mocks his chosen mode and the banality of its execution ('I have not spoken in riddles have I?': 1158). There is no way that Menelaus can come back with another fable after this. Teucer's pseudo-fable is a line longer than Menelaus' – the capping in length perhaps underlines Teucer's victory.

Teucer displays devastating wit in the *stichomythia* too. He leads Menelaus into an absurd claim at 1126: that Ajax has killed him. Now *we* know what Menelaus means, but Teucer is able to mock this face-value lie in a way which perhaps even raised a laugh from the audience (1127). At the end of the exchange, Teucer gets the last word: he easily caps Menelaus' final expression of shame that anyone should see him bandying words with Teucer when he has the power to use violence against him (1159-62). This mention of physical force, and the laughable assertion that he has been punishing Teucer with words, shows that Menelaus has lost the verbal contest. Spartans were supposed to be good at pithy one-liners – this is where we get the expression 'laconic' from.[35] Teucer has beaten Menelaus at his own national game.

As a dramatic *tour de force*, this exchange exemplifies the flexibility with which Sophocles handles tragic form and tone in order to develop character and thematic depth. The scholiast who condemned the duel as 'more at home in comedy' rather missed the point: tragic (and epic) contests between heroes are *allowed* to be coarse and amusing (Scholion on 1127).[36] Furthermore, this spat is a display of what Homerists, linguists and anthropologists call 'flyting' – that is, verbal duelling (sometimes in popular, improvised verse or song) with an *ad hominem* orientation.[37] Homeric heroes 'flyte' all the time, and in a highly nuanced and sophisticated fashion.[38] Menelaus' and Teucer's flyting also calls to mind the improvised exchanges of abusive and (sometimes) humorous verse – the *mandinadhes* – which play an important role in the assertion and display of manhood in the modern Cretan mountain community studied by Michael Herzfeld.[39] In both the Homeric and Cretan contexts, 'flyting' involves a mixture of the playful and the deadly serious – you win these contests with entertaining put-downs, but they are often a means of heading off physical violence via verbal humiliation. In Homer, they can also be a *prelude* to violence.

Teucer makes any recourse to violence on Menelaus' part seem unmanly and shameful but he has defeated the Spartan by drawing him into an entertaining game with rules of respon-sion. Teucer asserts his identity as a bowman in a way which speaks to and questions the 'hoplite' bias of Athenian military ideology: you don't have to be a shield-bearer like his brother to have worth and stature. And by beating up a king with *words* he is undermining the charge which Agamemnon will elaborate, namely that his foreignness and illegitimacy actually bastardise his language. Furthermore, Teucer will say to Agamemnon that he would rather die conspicuously (*prodêlôs*) while labouring on his brother's behalf than on behalf of Helen (1310-12). That reference to dying conspicuously, and while labouring, connects to Teucer's fear that Telamon will berate him for unmanliness. Teucer is attempting to perform his bravery and manhood as conspicuously and memorably as possible – to show that he flytes and hence *verbally fights* for his brother as a proper man should.[40] By making himself a big storm from a small cloud, through combative words and with creative brio, Teucer shows that a man can be brave and loyal without dying. He also shows that you can use words to fight cleverly as well as negotiate cleverly, the latter being Odysseus' forte in this play.

Supplication, cult and dreams of peace (1163-222)

When Menelaus exits and Tecmessa arrives with Eurysaces, Teucer orders the boy to touch his father's body 'as a suppliant' (1172). He must sit facing the corpse holding locks of hair from himself, his mother and Teucer (1175). Teucer then curses any warrior who should try to tear Eurysaces away from his father (1175-9). The Chorus are not to 'stand around like women': they must protect the boy as he clings to the body. Teucer then exits to make a grave 'though all the world forbids me' (1180-4).

These instructions and the silent stage business which accompanies them offer a moment of tranquil reverence for Ajax which contrasts with the previous shouting match. Our attention is now re-focused on the dead hero and his vulnerable heir. But Teucer also initiates two interdependent moments of ritual. First, Eurysaces protects the body through the ritual of supplication – to remove the body from the suppliant or vice versa would be to violate Zeus' protection, a very sacrilegious act. Secondly, the supplication, curse and offering of hair are three practices associated with the consecration of a hero in cult.[41] Thus, Eurysaces' supplication is another step in the play's narrative of Ajax's attainment of cultic status in Attica. Teucer activates the power of the hero's body and tomb: 'the dead hero, who a few moments ago was so helpless, is now, even before he is buried, in a position to protect his dependants and do harm to his enemies'.[42] But the on-stage tableau stresses that it is only his immediate family who draw on Ajax's power: we will have to wait longer for the benefits of his cult to be made open to *non-kin* – an important final phase in Ajax's journey towards integration as a hero of the Athenian polis.

That Athens is an end-point for Ajax's tragedy and everyone's suffering is emphasised by the Chorus in their third *stasimon*: they wish that they were in 'holy Athens' now that Ajax, their 'bulwark', is dead (1215-22). But these lyrics are not merely designed to flatter the audience. The Chorus wonder whether the 'unceasing bane of battle-toil' at Troy will ever end (1185-91). They wish Death on the man who first invented weapons and showed warfare to the Greeks (1192-8).[43] This inventor has deprived them of various forms of 'pleasure': primarily the garlands, wine and music of the symposium – all very *social* and *civilised* enjoyments. The Chorus have also lost proper sleep and the joy of sexual love (1199-205). Instead, they lie uncared for, their hair always sodden with dew and their thoughts full of 'baneful Troy' (1206-10). Heart-breakingly, they ask 'What pleasure will still be my portion?' (1215). As in other tragedies, the Chorus dream of going to a place which will deliver them from their present troubles.[44] This moving contrast between pleasure and war has to be set against the implicit glorifications of military self-sacrifice which pervaded polis life: Tyrtaeus' elegies, Athenian funeral speeches and the pre-play ceremonies of the City Dionysia itself. The Chorus are not directly attacking such glorifications with an 'anti-war' stance, but they *are* viewing war as a negation of civilised life's normal enjoyments. They remind the fifth-century citizen that his soldiering role can put an end to all the other pleasurable roles which define him.

This stress on the joys of society and sex also contrasts with

Ajax's grim desire for, and joy at, his own death (684-6, 966-7). Ajax's madness, isolation and savagery are a far cry from these social(ised) pleasures. But the Chorus also point to his status as protector. Indeed, the *stasimon* 'projects upon a larger screen the question of Ajax's isolation and relation to the life-affirming values of civilization' and beneath its various antitheses runs 'the deeper contrast' of Ajax's *double status*: suicide and saviour, criminal and victim, outcast and cult-hero.[45]

For all this doubleness, though, Ajax has left his loved ones behind. Throughout Teucer's speech and the Chorus's song, Tecmessa's mute presence reminds us of this fact. She will remain silent until the end of the play. Ajax had told her that 'silence adorns a woman'. Perhaps her silence now serves as a 'symbol of passive grief' and 'a dumb protest' against the self-important language of the men.[46]

Agamemnon and Teucer (1223-316)

Teucer races back on stage because Agamemnon is approaching. (Torn between the need to dig a grave and the need to protect Eurysaces and the corpse, we are meant to be impressed by his success in covering both tasks.) Agamemnon was probably played by the same actor who took Menelaus' part – after all, the brothers *are* peas in a (nasty) pod. We have to remember that Agamemnon is the supreme commander of the Greek army. His costume and bearing probably denoted this high status.

Status and speaking rights are immediately at issue: Teucer expects Agamemnon to unleash his 'foolish mouth' and the general cannot believe that a 'son of a captive woman' has dared to open *his* mouth in dissent (1225-30). He hurls Teucer's previous abuse of Menelaus back at him and his dead brother: he is a nobody speaking on behalf of a nobody (1231). Good birth (*eugeneia*) remains the point of contention: Agamemnon argues that Teucer did not have a 'noble mother' (*mêtros eugenous*: 1229). He rails at the suggestion that the Atreids have no authority over Ajax: 'are these not monstrous insults to hear from the mouths of slaves?' (1235). Menelaus was a snobbish dealer in half-truths but Agamemnon raises the stakes by claiming that Ajax and Teucer are *slaves*. He even asks Teucer to bring forward a 'free man' to plead Ajax's case because he does not understand Teucer's 'barbarian tongue' (1260-3). In Athenian law, slaves were not allowed to plead in court.

Like Menelaus, Agamemnon is behaving outrageously – *his* 'good birth' is freighted with prejudice and calumny. But Teucer beats him at this game: his long reply includes a coruscating deconstruction of Agamemnon's lineage (1289-97): he is a fool to raise questions of birth when his own grandfather, Pelops, was a barbarian. And what about Agamemnon's father (Atreus), who fed his brother the flesh of his own children? Then there was his Cretan mother – caught taking a lover to her bed. Can such a man as Agamemnon insult Teucer's pedigree? (1298). After all, Telamon won the 'highest prize' for valour and Hesione was a princess (1300-2). Proud of his noble family, Teucer would much rather die fighting for Ajax's burial than be killed in a war over Helen. In a cruel jibe he makes the deliberate slip of calling Helen the wife of Agamemnon before he corrects himself (1311-12). Again, Teucer exhibits wit and verve: Agamemnon's family is far more barbarian and savage than his. But this is not just another fine display of 'flyting'. It is a point-for-point refutation of Agamemnon in the style of an Athenian law-court oration or a sophistic display-speech (complete with clever manipulations of mythological examples).[47] Teucer is showing Agamemnon that he is Greek and free enough to outdo him in forensic pleading.

Teucer does not answer all the general's charges. But his response here is very important for understanding the play's relevance to its audience. Pericles' law of 451/0 stated that nobody could be a legitimate Athenian citizen unless both his parents were Athenian. Even if *Ajax* was performed before this law came into effect, Teucer's deconstruction of Agamemnon's 'Greekness' and 'nobility' speaks to (and perhaps questions) the exclusionist and elitist tendencies of Athenian civic ideology in particular and Hellenic chauvinism in general. This bastard-bowman's own good character and knock-down rhetoric undermine definitions of 'noble' character which rely too heavily on ethnicity or particular ancestral connections. Again, the audience are invited to look closely at their most deep-seated attitudes.

Of course it is not just the Atreids who betray definitions of 'good birth' which are too narrow and rigid. Ajax failed to see Tecmessa's point that his survival would be an act of *charis* and hence a truer act of *eugeneia* than death. Indeed, Teucer echoes this point directly when he berates Agamemnon for his lack of gratitude (*charis*) towards Ajax (1266-9). The Atreids' moral and social evaluations are extremely bankrupt but Teucer reminds us of Ajax's failings too.

Agamemnon has accused Teucer of *hubris*, but we feel again that hypocrisy and self-importance undermine the charge (1258). 'Will you not exercise *sôphrosunê*?' he demands (1259). This rather eerily echoes Ajax's (possibly sarcastic) claim that he will learn *sôphrosunê* in his deception speech, not to mention Athena's implication that Ajax is not *sôphrôn* (677, 132). Like Athena and Menelaus, Agamemnon has a debased, authoritarian view of this concept.

In the *Ajax*, *sôphrosunê* is a word which, despite its connotations of self-control, wisdom and moderation, is easily invoked to serve less-than-laudable moral and political outlooks.[48] Of course, it is true that Ajax's actions and Teucer's anger could be deemed as lacking in *sôphrosunê* on anybody's definition. But where Athenian texts often promote and appeal to *sôphrosunê* as a governing value for the ideal citizen, this play seems to show that immoderate language and behaviour might sometimes be justified in the face of tyranny, injustice and impiety. It also suggests that arrogant and authoritarian forces can hijack moral vocabulary for their own ends.

So the play encourages its audience to think carefully about attributions of *hubris* and *sôphrosunê* – these words' usage and meanings can be perverted. In this regard, Sophocles analyses the linguistic fall-out of intra-community conflict in a similar fashion to his contemporary Thucydides: when the historian describes the outbreak of civil war (*stasis*) in Corcyra, he notes that the warring parties 'exchanged their usual verbal evaluations for new ones ... thus irrational daring was considered courage and loyalty to one's party' (Thucydides 3.82.4). The historian adds, and this has particular resonance for our play, that *stasis* made 'any idea of moderation (*sôphrosunê*) just an attempt to disguise one's unmanly character'. He also says that conditions of factional conflict meant there was no place for 'an ability to understand all sides of a question'. Sophocles and Thucydides could both see that the exigencies of *stasis* create harmful changes in the way in which moral language is used and render intellectual virtue impotent.

Despite his brutal and repulsive attitude, Agamemnon does advance the case against Ajax in a way which gives pause for thought. He asks what kind of man (*anêr*) Ajax is (1236): a central question first posed by Athena and which persists throughout the play (77).[49] Agamemnon's point is that Ajax was not the only man in the Greek army to fight well (1237-8). Teucer will have a good answer for this: Ajax was the only warrior to stop Hector's rout and was prepared to face Hector in one-to-one combat – episodes which Agamemnon has conveniently forgotten (1273-87). But Teucer does not respond to Agamemnon's next point that a 'majority of judges' voted to award Achilles' arms to Odysseus (1243). What would happen if everyone behaved like Teucer when they lost a vote? Agamemnon's answer echoes his brother's fondness for political theory: 'No law could ever be soundly established' (1246). Now this point would be undermined if the play ever made it clear that the 'majority vote' was achieved corruptly – as both Ajax and Teucer have alleged (442-6, 1135). But Sophocles does not offer any corroboration for these allegations. The audience can only wonder whether the vote was free of 'sleaze'.

Agamemnon's argument should make us uneasy. If the majority of judges *genuinely* voted in favour of Odysseus, then surely Agamemnon is right to point out that majority verdicts must be accepted? How else can the rule of law in society be maintained? Teucer's silence on this issue is telling. Ajax may be an exceptional individual who protected his community but his individualistic claims to honour and recognition have ripped at the fabric which keeps a polis clothed in stability.

Odyssean virtue and models of masculinity (1273-420)

Despite Agamemnon's salient introduction of polis-friendly principles, Teucer's balancing account of his brother's battle-prowess is important for the final scenes' partial restoration of Ajax's reputation. Ajax's wretched isolation is refigured as singular and special heroism: 'he himself *alone* faced Hector *alone*' (1283).[50] Teucer is pointing out that Ajax did not fight simply for self-glorification: he fought as defender and champion of the entire Greek army.

Teucer is also constructing a defence of Ajax's style of masculinity. Agamemnon has argued that 'it is not burly or broad-backed men that are safest, but men of sound mind (*phronountes eu*) who are everywhere the best' (1250-1). Like everyone else, he invokes the imagery of 'big' and 'small': 'An ox may have big (*megas*) flanks, yet it is a small (*smikras*) whip that keeps it on the straight road' (1253-4). Agamemnon is arguing that brawn is no match for brains. The bulky machismo of Ajax is being set at naught, but Teucer counters that it served the Greek army very well.

Of course, the Ajax of Agamemnon's recollection jars with the display of intellect which the audience has seen in the deception speech. Ajax has complicated his own self-image just before his death: in theory at least, 'Odyssean' intellect and 'Ajaxian' ethos can be combined. Agamemnon is gesturing towards the unviability of Ajaxian masculinity in comparison with a fifth-century, polis-friendly and intellectual style of self-assertion.[51] This is a style which *Odysseus himself exhibits* and which – ironically – is not to Agamemnon's taste when he actually sees it working in favour of Ajax's proper burial (1316-73). Agamemnon's 'black and white' oppositions (past and present, brawn and brain) are ultimately shown to be too simplistic. For Odysseus' intelligent resolution of the impasse over Ajax's corpse is not a triumph of Odyssean 'brain' over Ajaxian 'brawn' in any straightforward sense. Rather, Odysseus' fulsome praise of Ajax as a warrior and his enactment of 'mutability' principles (which Ajax himself apprehended) signal the value of *both* models of masculinity. Having said this, the

124

Ajaxian ethos does not partake of cooperation, flexibility and mutability in the way that it perhaps should, and Odysseus' display of such virtues underlines this.

Teucer's role in giving Odysseus his due is telling in this regard. He acknowledges that a former enemy has acted contrary to expectation in defending Ajax's honour (1381-99). It is not that Teucer has suddenly put aside his extreme hostility to Ajax's enemies – he will pray that the Atreids be visited with horrible vengeance (1386-92). And he does not actually call Odysseus a 'friend'. But he stresses that he now sees Odysseus as *esthlos* ('good') and in doing so he mirrors Odysseus' 'flexibility'. Teucer's qualities thus emerge as neither fully Odyssean nor completely Ajaxian: he does not have Odysseus' skills in flexible thinking and is not a 'bulwark' of the army as Ajax was. But he shows a talent for survival and verbal combat. He is not intimidated by chauvinism and power-play. He succeeds in protecting his charges until Odysseus arrives. And he *is* flexible once he sees that Odysseus is acting as a friend.

If only Ajax could have combined such flexibility with his awesome fighting power! But Teucer has to refuse Odysseus' request that he help with the burial 'in case it brings displeasure to the dead' (1394-5). Teucer knows that his brother's spirit will always be implacable and inflexible. We can argue that Ajax's implacable ethos is a necessary component of his cult-heroic function. But this is very different from saying that Ajax's recent actions have been exonerated by Odysseus' intervention. Odysseus' and Teucer's 'coming to terms' indicates that, while Ajax's power, bravery and integrity are viable traits in a properly functioning community, his rigid attitude towards friendship and enmity, not to mention his violent reaction to perceived injustice, are not. Ajax could never have brought himself to act as Odysseus and Teucer do in the final scene of the play: he 'sustains from the grave the anti-cooperative role he played in life'.[52]

It should already be clear that Odysseus' intervention saves the day. He exemplifies a model of excellence which highlights the shortcomings of Ajax's ethos. But how does Odysseus actually secure the burial of Ajax in the face of Agamemnon's rigidity? As we saw in the prologue, Odysseus respects Ajax as a warrior, and this is again signalled as soon as he reappears: he asks why there is shouting over 'this brave corpse' (1319). Agamemnon tries to lay the blame on Teucer for abusing him. Odysseus wants to know who started the insults – he can forgive a man for responding in kind (1322-3). Agamemnon has to admit that he started the abuse but only because of what Teucer was *doing*. Odysseus is still wonderfully sceptical: 'What was it that he *did* to you, that resulted in actual injury?' (1325). Agamemnon has no *deeds* to report: Teucer has only *said* that he will defy Agamemnon by burying the body (1326-7).[53] Even before Odysseus explicitly parts company with Agamemnon's view of the situation, he exhibits what I have been calling 'intellectual virtue': he does not take Agamemnon's account at face-value and interrogates him with rigour and impartiality.

Having forced Agamemnon to divulge an accurate picture of what has been said, Odysseus goes further with his trademark cunning. To make his opinions more palatable he dwells on his status as Agamemnon's trusted *philos*: 'may a friend speak the truth and remain your partner no less than before?' (1328-9). Agamemnon actually responds well to this tactful rhetoric of *philia*: he says that he would be mad not to listen to a loyal friend. Then Odysseus delivers the bombshell (1332-46): '... by no means let violence force you into hating him so much that you trample on justice'. He admits that Ajax was 'the most hated man in the army' to him after the Judgement of Arms. Despite this hatred, Odysseus would never have denied that Ajax was 'the single most excellent man of all the Argives' excepting Achilles. If Agamemnon dishonours Ajax's body he will be destroying divine law. Furthermore, it is 'not just to harm the good man, if he should die, even if you happen to hate him'.

Odysseus' position is a significant advance on the attitudes and outlooks of all the other adult male characters.[54] Odysseus thinks you must be just to a good man regardless of whether or not he is your friend – this contrasts with Teucer at 1130-4. Odysseus does not think that the pursuit of justice permits the unlimited pursuit of personal revenge and this outlook is in contrast to that of Ajax and the Atreids. As Blundell puts it, Odysseus' justice is 'not simple retaliation, but the dispensation of honour according to personal worth'.[55] Thus he departs both from Ajax's anarchic and violent vision of absolute justice *and* the Atreids' pursuit of polis-based law and order – a pursuit which has no regard for divine law or basic human feeling. Odysseus also backs up his vision of justice and piety with persuasive rhetoric rather than violence or threats. This does not make Odysseus the Greek heroic counterpart of a modern liberal. His preparedness to stop hating Ajax is contingent upon the hero being dead and noble (1340-7). But he does seem to believe that Ajax should receive the recognition whose absence drove him to attempt murder in the first place. And he also seems to believe that this respect can transform enmity back into friendship.

Agamemnon will not be persuaded to respect Ajax or regard him as a friend. Nor will he agree that burying the body is the right thing to do. But he *is* persuaded to let the burial take place. Odysseus achieves this shift by emphasising three ideas: nobility, mutability (in *philia*) and flexibility of outlook. These ideas emerge through some clever rhetorical parrying of Agamemnon's objections and a continued appeal to the friendship that exists between Odysseus and the king. When Agamemnon objects that Ajax was insubordinate, Odysseus says he is the 'winner' when 'conquered by friends' (1353). The king should focus on what will please his *philos*. Still not grasping Odysseus' point, Agamemnon says he cannot show respect and *charis* towards the corpse of an enemy (1354, 1356). Odysseus retorts that Ajax's nobility and excellence (*aretê*) outweigh enmity (1355, 1357). But, Agamemnon says, people like Ajax are 'unstable among mortals' (1358). Odysseus agrees that 'many who are now friends turn out later unpleasant' and in so doing he echoes the 'insight' of Ajax in the deception speech (1359, 678-83). When Agamemnon implies that such changeable friends are no friends at all, Odysseus cleverly stresses the undesirability of an 'unyielding soul' (*sklêran psuchên*: 1361). In so doing, he uses vocabulary which had been applied to Ajax's rigidity and Teucer's harshness (649, 1119).

127

Odysseus thus stresses the similarity between Ajax and Agamemnon. But the difference with Agamemnon is that he does at least succumb to Odysseus' rhetoric of *philia*. He will allow Ajax to be buried because Odysseus wishes it and Odysseus is his friend (1370-3). But he exits the scene without in any way accepting that Ajax is excellent, that the burial is just or that friendship is mutable and transient. For Agamemnon, the burial is Odysseus' deed, not his (1368).

Odysseus then sets about capitalising on the fact that he has just won Ajax's burial by offering friendship to the dead hero's dependants. Again, his language is a deliberate echo of Ajax's deception speech: Odysseus wants Teucer to be his friend 'to the same extent' that he was previously his enemy (1376-80). Teucer is guardedly positive and although he cannot allow Odysseus to take full part in the burial, he wants him to help out (1395-6). But it is not just the value of flexibility and change which this rapprochement exemplifies. Teucer says: 'Most excellent Odysseus, I can give you only praise when you speak; you have deceived me greatly in my expectation' (1381-2). Aside from the obvious joke that the proverbially duplicitous and cunning Odysseus has once again deceived *by being honest*, these lines offer another example of the play's concern with dashed expectation and revised understanding. In the same way that the Chorus and Tecmessa realise too late that they were duped by Ajax's professed change of heart and wish they had understood the situation better, Teucer highlights the fact that Odysseus' character has been misunderstood. Throughout the play Ajax and his *philoi* assume that Odysseus is mocking their predicament and is ready to rain laughter and *hubris* upon them. They cast him in the role of 'worst enemy' when he actually respects them and is prepared to defend a form of justice and *sôphrosunê* which benefits and gives due respect to all parties: even the Atreids are beneficiaries because they have been prevented from acting impiously.

What the audience sees here is that prejudice and partiality have led to false character-assessments and corrosive division. Again, the tragedy uses audience-generated irony in order to display the difficulty of achieving correct understanding while at the same time showing the need for, and benefits, of such intellectually virtuous striving (in the form of Odysseus' even-handedness).

Does Odysseus' intellectual virtue and the success he has in performing it make him the real hero of the play? Are Odysseus' excellence in argument, flexibility and the rhetoric of 'mutability' shown to be better than Ajax's intransigence and splendid isolation? Are we being shown that Odysseus did really deserve the arms of Achilles after all? Or are we meant to see Odysseus' virtue as engendering the sorts of compromise which are useful in some contexts but treacherous in others? Doesn't Ajax's (and Agamemnon's) point still stand: friends who turn into enemies are no friends at all? Aren't 'mutability' and 'flexibility' mere 'spin' for betrayal?

To some extent these are questions which every audience-member and every reader has had to decide for herself.[56] But it is not clear to me that Sophocles is loading the text strongly either way. As Blundell points out, any reading which seeks to decide which of the two heroes is shown to be better in the play rather assumes that Ajax's and Odysseus' differing *aretai* ('excellences') can be measured against each other.[57] The play seems to suggest the reverse: the virtues of the two heroes are incommensurable and each has its place. For example, we are told that the criterion for the 'Judgement of Arms' was who had the 'most excellent hand' (*aristocheir*: 934). Odysseus deserves to win such a contest only if this apparent criterion of physical prowess is supplanted or supplemented with an appeal to cunning and intellectual skills. But the play shows that there was no agreement on what the criterion of the 'Judgement' should be or else how it should have been interpreted. Hence there can be no solution to the quarrel between Ajax and his enemies. For his part, Teucer acknowledges that *both* heroes are the 'best' and in doing so, he perhaps shows his own (third) kind of excellence and stature (1381, 1415).

Ajax's and Odysseus' differing styles of masculinity and excellence may well be incommensurable. And Agamemnon's convenient simplifications may have perhaps led critics to forget Ajax's 'Odyssean' side. Ajax's delusions, uncertain mental state and the opacities of the deception speech make it dangerous to even try to evaluate him as a consistent character. Nevertheless, the final debate-scenes and Odysseus' intervention offer a range of 'models' of masculinity and 'criteria' for judging a man's worth which would have led a specifically fifth-century Athenian audience to question their own normative standards of judging character and virtue. Teucer's aggressive wit and fearless loyalty show that high status, ethnicity and good birth are not always necessary or sufficient criteria for attributing worth and good character. Agamemnon, Menelaus and Ajax demonstrate that arrogance and rigidity may block the proper perfomance of social goods such as gratitude, *sôphrosunê* and piety. Odysseus shows that an awareness of flexibility and mutability need not undermine justice, *philia* or social bonds. Ajax's awesomeness as a warrior is figured as community-saving. But the criterion of polis-friendliness exposes his excessive self-regard and dangerous indiscipline.

In these and other ways, the quarrelling-scenes *do* effect a 'rehabilitation' of Ajax *and* a 'showcase' for Odysseus' enlightened heroism. But to describe the play's last third simply in terms of this dual function hardly does justice to the deliberately messy and complicated way in which *all* the male characters involved add to and subtract from Ajax's good name. Teucer, Odysseus and even the Atreids nuance our sense of Ajax's qualities and shortcomings and deepen our idea of the skills and virtues which a man needs in the social world beyond the battlefield.

7

Criticism and Reception

Heroism and character

In this final chapter, I want to assess some of the views of the play which have been implicit or explicit in the previous chapters. I will also look briefly at some post-Sophoclean representations of Ajax the hero and *Ajax* the play in order to highlight the way in which modern criticism on *Ajax* is always, at least in part, mediated by artists and thinkers who have recast the mythic and dramatic material so that it speaks to their own concerns and cultures. We saw that the *Ajax* 'recasts' Homeric epic and other instantiations of myth in ways which emphasise the hero's difficult status in terms of fifth-century institutions and values. Sophocles has not been immune to such 'recasting' himself. Readers, critics and writers cannot prevent their interpretations of ancient myth and literature from being infused with contemporary concerns or being shaped by received trends and ideas which are themselves products of earlier acts of recasting. This does not mean that it is impossible or wrong to ask what this play meant to its original audience. But we should always look at the way in which past scholarship and other artistic or intellectual responses have shaped our reading of the 'original' play.

Critics have always seen something distinctive about Sophocles' heroes in comparison with those of Homer, Aeschylus or Euripides. The idea of a generalised 'Sophoclean hero' has made frequent appearances in scholars' assessments.[1] It is much harder to encapsulate (or plausibly generalise towards) an 'Aeschylean hero' or 'Euripidean hero', and this says something about the way in which the extant Sophoclean tragedies are consistently focused on single, isolated figures. But essentialising an author's characters in this way can be the literary-critical equivalent of social stereotyping: we emphasise the similarities between groups of characters and downplay the differences between them. We must try not to force Ajax to conform to a general concept of heroism which is nothing more than a critical mirage – a product of our fondness for finding pithy ways to sum up an artist's thematic and aesthetic signature.

Furthermore, the idea that Sophoclean heroes are distinctive and share a kind of brand identity is complicit with other potentially distorting assumptions. Here are two of them:

1. That a tragic drama has to have *a* hero or *one* hero who is 'great'.
2. That this hero has a 'character' or 'personality' which is the same as that of figures in a modern realist novel or drama or a real person we know.

The first assumption derives from chapter 13 of Aristotle's *Poetics*, where the best type of tragic plot seems to require a dramatic concentration on a single, central figure.[2] Other Aristotelian statements about tragic agency stress the importance of close (often intra-familial) relationships *between* characters from heroic myth. And Aristotle's ideal plots seem to allow a focus on the agency of characters other than the primary hero(ine).[3] But these qualifications have been sidelined in favour of seeing tragedies as focused on a single hero or main character. Of course, assumption 1 works for *Ajax* better than it does for some other tragedies. Ajax is undoubtedly a dominant figure on whom characters, Chorus and audience are nearly always focused: even after his death, his corpse and past life directs the action and arguments. But we saw that the Atreids, Teucer and Odysseus offered examples of action and attitude which were something more than mere tools for deepening our positive and negative judgements and concerns about Ajax. In particular, Teucer becomes a focal character in his own right and the positive and intelligent interventions of Tecmessa and the superior justice of Odysseus also make it hard to read *Ajax* as 'about' Ajax alone.

It is beyond the scope of this book to unpack the second assumption thoroughly. But a sketch of the problem is essential. In the past two hundred years, Romantic ideas have been grafted onto Aristotle's *Poetics* in order to support the critical notion that Greek tragedy is primarily concerned with tragic heroes with very human characters and 'flaws'.[4] But Aristotle wrote that tragedy is an imitation of action and life rather than people (*Poetics* 1450a16f.). And he argued that *êthos* (which we must translate as 'character' without committing to modern notions of 'character') is revealed by the deliberate moral choices which tragic figures make manifest in words or deeds. For Aristotle, 'there is no *êthos* in those speeches in which there is nothing at all that the speaker chooses or rejects' and he can even conceive of a tragedy that has no *êthos* in it at all (*Poetics* 1450b8-10, 1450a16-39). Now these ideas are specifically informed by Aristotle's wider moral-philosophical framework. But they do illustrate the point that *êthos* does not necessarily attempt to express 'a whole personality or the make-up of a psyche' as 'character' does in modern usage.[5] Indeed, as Stephen Halliwell remarks, Aristotle's subordination of *êthos* to action is very different to the 'post-Romantic belief in the centrality of psychological characterisation' in literature.[6]

When we read the *Ajax*, then, we may inevitably bring anachronistic and excessively 'realist' conceptions of character to it: we might be looking for consistency, 'completeness' and deep motivations in the characters which are not there. Jones argued that there is a lack of 'inwardness' to characters like Ajax which is figured in the convention of the tragic mask: 'its being is exhausted in its features'.[7] And Taplin once wrote that 'the revelation of psychology is only incidental to a scene's primary dramatic purpose'.[8] But how true is all this? It is certainly tempting to use such outlooks to side-step the controversies over whether Ajax *really* intends to deceive or whether or not he has *really* changed his mind in the deception speech. And it is undeniable that conventions of tragic-poetic diction and 'set-piece' structures like the *agôn* and *stichomythia* make tragic characterisation very different from modern novelistic characterisation. But ambiguities, uncertainties and gaps of motive in tragedy have great dramatic potential and may betoken a fairly realistic representation of life's complex causations and the problems we have in interpreting other minds.[9] Sophocles' characters *are* humanly intelligible and the playwright does evince an interest in the inner life of a person – we keep seeing that Ajax's 'inner life', although elusive and mysterious, is very much at issue in our play. John Gould pointed out that neither ancient nor modern conceptions of fiction are naively 'realist' about character anyway – who ever thought that conceptions of self, personhood and continuity of character were straightforward?[10] Goldhill actually uses Ajax's uncertain state of mind to illustrate his point that tragedy effects 'transgressions and dislocations of the self' and that any reading of the play which treats modern conceptions of 'character' or 'human nature' or 'what any person feels' as eternal verities will distort its culturally specific and very complex presentation of mind, motivation and character.[11]

The debate about tragic characterisation is ongoing.[12] But it should now be apparent that approaches to the *Ajax* which focus on the 'psychology' of its central figure *qua* 'tragic' or 'Sophoclean hero' may contain a number of assumptions which have 'recast' or – less neutrally – *distorted* classical conceptions of tragic agency and character.

Nevertheless, the idea that all the extant Sophoclean tragedies share a *similar* vision of heroism has much to recommend it. It is true that 'each of Sophocles' surviving plays is dominated by a figure or figures who attempt to live out a pattern of heroic belief in the face of extended opposition'.[13] For Bernard Knox – whose work on Sophocles has done so much to make plausible the notion of a distinctively *Sophoclean* hero – figures like Ajax, Philoctetes, Electra and Antigone all reject limitations on human stature. They all refuse to yield to others or to be persuaded out of their beliefs and commitments. For Knox, the 'Sophoclean hero' is markedly stubborn: 'it is difficult to tell him anything at all: he will not surrender'. Any attempt to curb or sway the

Sophoclean hero or heroine provokes their ire: 'they are all angry heroes'. Their rigidity of belief and purpose means that they 'defy time and its imperative of change'.[14] Alongside this refusal to relent or change, the Sophoclean hero(ine) exhibits a 'death wish'. Knox's take on the 'Sophoclean hero' is neatly and powerfully summarised thus:

> Immovable once his decision is taken, deaf to appeals and persuasion, to reproof and threat, unterrified by physical violence, even by the ultimate violence of death itself, more stubborn as his violation increases until he has no one to speak to but the unfeeling landscape, bitter at the disrespect and mockery the world levels at what it regards as failure, the hero prays for revenge and curses his enemies as he welcomes death that is the predictable end of his intransigence.

Knox, Heroic Temper, p. 44

This summary captures Sophocles' Ajax to some extent. But there are a number of points in Knox's general formulation of Sophoclean heroism which are not perfectly applicable to Ajax or whose applicability is challenged by certain readings which we have already entertained.

First, is Ajax 'unyielding'? To a great extent, yes: he commits suicide despite the appeals of Tecmessa and curses his enemies in the process. But we have seen that he does show some understanding of her arguments and does take account of certain elements of her case. He makes sure that Eurysaces will have a guardian who is not 'loveless' (Teucer) and in stressing that his son must care for his grandparents, Ajax shows that he has acknowledged and understood some of the family-based obligations which Tecmessa brings up. To be sure, he has only provided surrogates for himself, but this is hardly the mark of a character who is *completely* 'deaf to appeals and persuasion'.

I have discussed Christopher Gill's reading of the deception speech as a powerful articulation and reaffirmation of his exemplary gesture of suicide.[15] On this reading, Ajax is not ultimately 'unyielding' in a pejorative sense: his suicide is rationally and reflectively arrived at in response to improper treatment. His 'unyielding' characteristics thus stem from a sense of injustice rather than an individualistic refusal to bend to reasonable and fair social obligations or expectations. By contrast, Knox's stress on the stubborn nature of the Sophoclean hero pushes us towards seeing that hero as the *enemy* of reason and justice. In this respect, Knox's viewpoint has affinities with the 'pietist' approach defended by Winnington-Ingram.[16] Where Knox and Winnington-Ingram see Ajax as a transgressive figure, Gill is rehabilitating what Winnington-Ingram called a 'hero-worshipping' approach to the play. By seeing Ajax as a figure who is *wronged* before he does wrong himself, Gill attacks an assumption that Ajax's rigidity must be bad. Gill focuses on the causes and exact rationale for his 'unyielding' character. Knox's template for Sophoclean heroes comes close to assuming that Ajax's 'unyielding' *êthos* is part of his 'nature'. Gill sees Ajax's intransigence much less as an inevitable part of his nature and much more as a strategic response to the Judgement of Arms and the slaughter of the cattle. Of course, the question of how far Ajax's actions are to be read as typical of his nature or else as temporary and contingent lies at the heart of the tragedy – and it is not clear that the conundrum is (meant to be) solvable. But notice how Knox is veering towards a view of character as 'psychological make-up' and 'essential nature' while Gill is taking Ajax's character as an effect of the choices he makes and the reasons for those choices. Knox is being slightly post-Romantic while Gill is being slightly Aristotelian.[17] And these different approaches are yielding different levels and kinds of sympathy for Ajax – indeed they create readings of the play which are in many respects opposed to each other.

Madness, sanity and extremism

Knox's general definition of the 'Sophoclean hero' also elides specific and peculiar identities and states of mind which different Sophoclean protagonists display. Crucially, Ajax is the *only* extant Sophoclean character who is explicitly visited with delusions from a god. We have already seen that it is hard to determine quite how mad or deluded Ajax is throughout the play. To what extent and at what points we are meant to see him as regaining his wits is controversial. But for the other characters and the audience alike, Ajax's state of mind and the question of whether he is 'himself' are recurrent and troubling issues. To illustrate these issues and their impact on Ajax's tragedy is no small task. But a good sense of the play's presentation of them can be gained by reconsidering the first exchange which occurs between the Chorus and Tecmessa as they struggle to make sense of Ajax's behaviour and the second entrance of Ajax which follows that exchange (201-482).[18]

Tecmessa makes it clear that Ajax was 'seized by madness' (*maniai halous*: 216). Not for the last time, she glosses this madness as an illness (207). She informs the Chorus that Ajax is now *phronimos*: 'sane' (Garvie) or 'in his right mind' (Dutta). Ajax is now recovered from his 'sickness' but is instead vexed by 'sore grief' or 'evil pain' (274-5). Again and again, we find that words with the root *phron-* in them are used to characterise Ajax's state of mind.

Tecmessa goes on to tell of Ajax's struggle to understand why he is sitting surrounded by the carnage of dead animals. We have already discussed her description of the lamentations which she has never heard from him before (319-20). She is stressing that Ajax is doing something which goes against his usual 'character': although he is supposedly 'sane' again, he is no longer acting in accordance with his own ideals and standards. If Ajax is no longer actually deluded and if Tecmessa is right to feel that he is returned to sanity, what are we to make of her comments on his uncharacteristic behaviour? Even if he is now of 'sound mind', his wife draws attention to the fact that it is difficult to characterise him as 'himself'. The extent to which Ajax could be said to be 'sane' or restored to his 'normal' self is thus made uncertain for the audience.

The Chorus respond by saying 'terrible are the misfortunes which have driven the man frantic' (331-2). The word for 'driven ... frantic' here is *diapephoibasthai*, a compound verb not found anywhere else in extant Greek literature. Its etymology suggests that it should describe someone who is possessed by the god Phoebus Apollo but is used here in a more 'general sense'.[19] However, others have wanted to retain the sense of being brought to a state of 'spirit possession' or 'mantic ecstasy' implied by the verb, rather than watering it down to 'driven mad' or 'frenzied'.[20] Much of Ajax's most recent behaviour (his trance-like condition and change of voice) is consistent with the behaviour of figures like Cassandra who become possessed by Apollo's gift of prophecy. But Ajax is *not* really in a mantic state; he merely has coincidental symptoms. Nevertheless, the Chorus may be making a specific point that a malign power has taken *permanent possession* of his mind: 'the mental trouble outlasts the frenzy'.[21] This way, the Chorus believe that Ajax remains under some influence which affects his sanity or character. Again, as the Chorus and Tecmessa discuss Ajax's behaviour, we only gain further possibilities and uncertainties as to how his state of mind should be characterised.

When the hero is heard (from offstage) crying out inarticulately, the Chorus equivocates on Ajax's mental state (337-8). But as Ajax starts to use recognisable words, the Chorus becomes more certain that he is sane (*phronein*: 344). Then again, as soon as they actually see the hero surrounded by slaughtered animals, the Chorus leader reverts to ascriptions of insanity (354-5). As Ajax reflects angrily on his humiliation, Tecmessa tells him to come to his senses (*phronêson eu*: 371).[22] Ajax may be out of his frenzied state, but there is a question mark as to how sensible, sane or normal he is. As Goldhill puts it, 'the chorus' concern for Ajax's present and past state of sanity, and Ajax's own recognition of his mental and visual aberration place considerable emphasis on the uncertain questioning of the boundaries of normality with regard to Ajax's state of mind and behaviour. The return towards sanity weaves uncertainty around the precise boundary between madness and reason.'[23]

Goldhill rightly argues that the *Ajax's* complicated staging of 'character' and (in)sanity goes beyond the observation that Ajax's state of mind is often uncertain in the play. Ajax's 'madness' also provokes questions about the extent of his free will and autonomy. When Ajax reflects at length on the disgrace that has befallen him, he makes it clear that *he* feels no regrets about his original plan to murder the Atreids (447-9). Ajax may not be in his right mind when he says this, but he is unrepentant and adamant about the fact that he intended to do the crime before delusions deflected him. At the same time, he also acknowledges that Athena has controlled his actions: 'the Gorgon-eyed unconquerable goddess, inflicted on me the disease of madness (*lussôdê noson*) and tripped me up' (452). Ajax's state of mind during and after his frenzied attack is difficult to secure and we also find it difficult *either* to argue that Ajax was an entirely autonomous agent free from outside determining forces *or* to see his mind, intentions and actions as completely controlled or overdetermined by external divine forces. As Ajax struggles to make sense of his senses during the previous night's terrible events, the audience are treated to a tour of the complexities of internal and external causation, and the problems of determining the boundary between the two. They are also forced by the twists and turns of other characters' reactions to Ajax – and by the hero's own shifts in self-description and outward behaviour – to reflect and question the boundaries between reason and madness, between self-determination and fate.

More could be said about Ajax's character in relation to notions of sanity and autonomy.[24] But my preceding discussion should make it clear that Sophocles' exploration and presentation of Ajax's ambiguous mental state and Athena's affect on him is important and not easily assimilable to any general formulation of 'Sophoclean heroism'. Ajax's anger may be real and his attitude implacable, but the intervention of Athena lends a certain ambiguity to that bitterness and inflexibility: is Ajax's movement towards suicide ultimately an outcome of *his* character and intentions? Would he be behaving in this way if Athena had not decided to affect his mind? To be sure, Ajax's rage might lead us to conclude that he was unhinged *before* Athena interfered. But we cannot ignore the fact that Ajax's sanity is explicitly and constantly questioned throughout the play and that such uncertainties over the state of his mind must qualify and frame attempts to characterise Ajax as if he is straightforwardly 'flawed', entirely 'himself' or consistent in his outlook and intentions.

Knox views Sophocles' Ajax as 'the last of the heroes': 'his death is the death of the old Homeric (and especially Achillean) individual ethos which had for centuries of aristocratic rule served as the dominant ideal of man's nobility and action but which, by the fifth century, had been successfully challenged and largely superseded'.[25] For Knox, the strength and frequency of references to Homeric language, episodes and situations in the play are there to cast Ajax as an outdated Homeric hero. Thus the play opposes Homeric values to a more modern fifth-century ethic of self-control (*sôphrosunê*). This ethic is exemplified most starkly by Odysseus' rhetoric in the final scenes. Ajax's greatness is in conflict with more 'modern' ideals.

We have seen repeatedly that the language often used of and around Ajax explicitly recalls descriptions of him in the *Iliad* and *Odyssey*. Ajax is imbued with the discourse and values of Homer's heroes. It has even been argued that the *Ajax* explores 'ethical tensions within heroism which are strikingly similar to those of the *Iliad*' and that these are 'live issues' rather than poetic constructs.[26]

But we have also found that there are differences between Sophocles' Ajax and his Homeric counterparts. One of the most important differences lies in his attitude towards the gods. In contrast to Ajax's reported dismissal of divine aid and his contention that such aid diminishes a warrior's reputation (*kleos*) at 758-79, the warriors of the *Iliad* clearly regard victories attained *with* divine aid as more glorious than those attained without it. As Winnington-Ingram puts it: 'Ajax – and Ajax alone, the Sophoclean Ajax, feels that it would derogate from his prestige to accept help from a god ... Ajax rejects that sense of dependence upon the gods by which the pride of a Homeric hero is normally mitigated'.[27] Even the Homeric Achilles puts his anger aside having initially refused to restore the body of Hector to the Trojans. We get no comparable gesture of compromise or abatement from the Sophoclean Ajax:

'Achilles finally yields. Ajax in Sophocles' play rejects even that sense of final mitigation in his unforgiving, cursing suicide'.[28] Rather than think of Sophocles' Ajax as 'Homeric', it would be more accurate to describe him as 'hyper-Homeric'; he does not simply embody or iterate an epic model, but is a 'specific depiction, distorted in its extremism'.[29] This 'extremism' may not be properly understood without remembering that our play dramatises Ajax's journey towards cult-heroic status. It seems to be essential to their pedigree that cult-heroes suffer injustice, exhibit extreme qualities and achieve isolation. But this does not necessarily make Ajax's extremism palatable or unproblematic for an Athenian audience.

Does Ajax commit *hubris*?

It should be clear by now that critics have found it hard to agree on the balance of Ajax's positive and negative characteristics. This lack of consensus is compounded when the problem is framed in terms of *hubris*. In common parlance we apply the adjective 'hubristic' to a human attitude or action which might incur the anger or jealousy of the gods. And in classical scholarship *hubris* has often been thought to be the presumption or pride which causes a person to cross the line that should separate men from gods. It is this religious and theological aspect to *hubris* which has often been used to characterise the Sophoclean Ajax: some critics have argued that Ajax dies because he offends Athena.[30]

Neither ancient Greek culture nor our own play, however, define *hubris* in purely religious or theological terms. In archaic Greek poetry (especially Theognis and Solon), elite classical prose and the democratic oratory of Athens, *hubris* is often explicitly or implicitly opposed to the key moral and social concept of *sôphrosunê* (self-control, moderation, 'sound-mindedness'). Thus *hubris* can be the mark of excessive behaviour which is unbecoming to any good Greek citizen. An act of *hubris* usually seems to involve the 'deliberate infliction of shame and dishonour on another, often for the purpose of expressing a sense of superiority, or the drive to engage in such behaviour'.[31]

Hubris is 'often, but by no means necessarily, an act of violence' and is likely to 'lead to anger and attempts at revenge'.[32] The term is sometimes attributed to tyrants in archaic and classical literature, and this attribution gains particular strength in the specifically democratic (and often rabidly anti-tyrannical) context of fifth-century Athens. As the Chorus of elders put it in Sophocles' *Oedipus Tyrannus*: '*hubris* breeds the tyrant' (872). Excessive and competitive behaviour designed to assert superiority and humiliating shame upon a fellow citizen is often defined as *hubris* in democratic Athens and, while anyone can be accused of it, civic and political *hubris* is mainly attributed to the excessive acts committed by the powerful against the less powerful in our written sources.[33] In Athenian law and forensic oratory, *hubris* connotes a physically violent outrage committed by one citizen against the body of another. And such acts were rhetorically hyped into attacks on the integrity of the democratic body as a whole.[34] The law against *hubris* seemed to cover all the more serious assaults done a person (including what we would call 'grievous bodily harm'), and was remedied by public indictment.[35] However, it is clear that *hubris* can take the form of verbal insults as much as physical abuse. *Hubris* describes individual actions or a more general disposition of excessive self-assertion.[36]

There are five actual or intended actions in the play which are described as *hubris* by one character or another: (1) Ajax sees the award of arms to Odysseus as *hubris*. (2) Both he and his supporters expect further *hubris* (complete with laughter and humiliating mockery) from their enemies. (3) In turn, the Atreids think of Ajax's attempted revenge as *hubris* against them. (4) They think the same of attempts to recognise his status and bury his body. (5) Ajax's supporters think that the Atreids' refusal to bury Ajax is *hubris*.[37]

Allied to these accusations and discussions of *hubris* are all the play's references to 'thinking big' and 'talking big'. Menelaus shows that the line between full-blown and reprehensible *hubris* and mere 'talking big' and 'thinking big' can become imperceptible. Ajax's 'thinking' and 'talking' 'big' is what defines him but it becomes a worry for his supporters. Teucer's 'thinking big' seems to suggest that certain forms of self-assertion and aggressive performance are justifiable, crucially *distinct* from *hubris*, and that they can even be used to combat it. Indeed, the play's frequent use of *hubris*-words and its focus on talk and thoughts which are *megas* constitute a complex meditation on the shifting relations and uncertain limits between assertive language and thought which are legitimate and those actions and words which go beyond the pale because they inflict gratuitous injury and insult or twist revenge and punishment into excessive humiliation. Perhaps we should view *Ajax* as a play which dramatises the damage that *hubris* and talk about *hubris* can do to groups and individuals and accept that this dramatisation resists any definitive characterisation of Ajax as hubristic (or not).

Even so, it would be good to get some sense of how far the charge of *hubris* sticks to our central character in Athenian terms. At first sight, it seems obvious that Ajax has committed 'religious' *hubris*. We are explicitly told by the messenger that he rejected Athena's help in battle and is reported to have belittled the concept of the hero-warrior who needs divine aid (762-79). Surely it is this haughty, hubristic attitude which leads Athena to delude and apparently punish Ajax? Here are Athena's instructions to Odysseus in the opening scene (127-32):

> Look then on such things, and never speak yourself any arrogant word (*huperkopon epos*) against the gods, nor be puffed up with self-importance, if you outweigh someone else in might or in the depth of your great wealth. For a day can cause all human affairs to sink and bring them up again; it is the sound-minded (*sôphronas*) whom the gods love, while they hate the wicked (*kakous*).

Here, it seems that Athena is indeed holding up Ajax as an example of religious or theological *hubris*: she implies a contrast between arrogance towards the gods and sound-mindedness/self-control (*sôphrosunê*). By saying 'look on such things' to Odysseus, it is easy to come to the conclusion that Athena views Ajax's humiliation and her part in it as punishments for his hubristic 'puffed up' behaviour. If we put Athena's comments next to the messenger's report of Calchas' words, it seems as if the play is making an example of Ajax: hubristic behaviour (especially in relation to the gods) will have terrible consequences for the perpetrator.

But is the play's treatment of Ajax that simple? Garvie argues that there is nothing in the text of the *Ajax* to suggest that the audience are being led to associate the hero with religious *hubris*. Neither the messenger's report nor Athena's proclamation make mention of the word *hubris*. Nowhere in the tragedy is the word used to describe Ajax's attitude to the gods. Garvie concedes that some of the vocabulary which Athena uses is frequently associated with *hubris*. Ajax's first appearance certainly reveals him to be boastful and lacking in self-control. And 'the idea that excessive power or wealth may lead to *hubris* is a very common one'.[38] Nevertheless, continues Garvie, we should not accept Athena's interpretation without question:

> The quality for which Athena condemns Ajax is the one that Sophocles intends us to admire in him. The Sophoclean hero is never *sôphrôn*, but excessive in everything that he/she does. It is the ordinary, little people who advocate *sôphrosunê*.
>
> Garvie, *Ajax*, p. 136

On this reading, Athena's (and Menelaus') definition of *sôphrosunê* and any concomitant imputation of *hubris* is a reprehensible manipulation of moral vocabulary. It is also a foil to Odysseus' embodiment of the concept's true meaning. It can also be argued that Athena's words are too vague and leave Ajax's offence against her undefined. If Ajax has been generally guilty of *hubris*, why has her anger erupted on this particular occasion? Nowhere in the play are we told that Athena was angry because Ajax wanted to attack his enemies. Finally, Athena can be accused of inconsistency: 'the "moral" that the gods love the good and punish the evil is undercut by 131-2, where we learn that *all* human life is subject to falling and rising'.[39]

Even if we accept all of this, we still have to contend with the
apparently hubristic picture of Ajax which is provided by the
messenger's speech later in the play. Calchas says explicitly that
Ajax's boasts and his rejection of divine aid have provoked
Athena's fury (758-79). For many scholars, Calchas' interpretation explains Ajax's downfall: he has committed *hubris* by
failing to recognise his limitations and by not living in accordance with his human status. Like Teiresias in both *Antigone*
and *Oedipus Tyrannus*, Calchas is an important reminder of
'the limits set by the human condition, limits that the gods both
symbolise and enforce'.[40]

For Garvie, Calchas reports foolish, but not hubristic, acts on
Ajax's part. Sophocles does not use the term *hubris* to describe
Ajax's attitude towards the gods and the hero himself does not
blame Athena for his sufferings. He only blames the Atreids
(838). The word *hubris* and its cognates are mostly used (nine
times) to describe the actual or anticipated behaviour of Ajax's
enemies towards him or his son. Only twice is *hubris* definitely
used of Ajax's behaviour towards his enemies (1061, 1081). In
both of these cases, it is Menelaus who is speaking but we have
seen that Menelaus is an unattractive character who is fast
becoming a *hubristês* himself (1092).

There is one more instance where Tecmessa seems to be
describing Ajax as madly revelling in the *hubris* he thinks he
has paid back to the Atreids (304). However, the line is
ambiguous as to whether he sees himself as inflicting vengeful
hubris or merely vengeance *for* the *hubris* he feels that
Odysseus and the Atreids have committed against him. It may
convey both ideas. In which case, we *do* have an example of Ajax
admitting to *hubris* in the play. But Garvie is right to stress that
the tragedy never offers a *disinterested* view of Ajax as a
hubristês by using the relevant Greek word and its cognates. He
is also right that this word is never explicitly used to describe
Ajax's attitude towards the gods.

However, we should note that Menelaus does connect Ajax's
hubris with a god's behaviour: 'but as things are a god has
turned his outrageous behaviour (*hubris*) so that it fell on
sheep and herds' (1060-1). The line mentioning *hubris* as the

object of the god's changeful intervention may not be genuine.[41] And of course, the unpleasant Menelaus would say this – we do not have to agree with him. But if it is a genuine line, Menelaus stresses that Ajax has attempted homicidal assault on men who should be *philoi*. Furthermore, Menelaus has been present during (although not immediately party to) Calchas' prophecy and narration of the two occasions where Ajax has scorned divine support (750). So, when Menelaus characterises Ajax's failed mission as resulting from a divine deflection of *hubris* we are perhaps meant to think that he has gained intelligence of Calchas' confidential conversation with Teucer and sees it as having a bearing on the reasons why Ajax fell on the wrong target.

But there is a further problem in seeing Ajax as religiously hubristic. Fisher argues that *hubris* is not (as is traditionally assumed) primarily a religious offence committed by a human being against the gods or the presumption or pride which leads a person to transgress the line that should separate men from gods.[42] *Hubris* describes violent, dishonourable and shame-causing behaviour committed by one human against another. The victims of *hubris* naturally hope that the gods will avenge such behaviour, as with all offences against morality, but that does not turn it into a peculiarly religious offence, even in the few cases where the *hubris* seems to be primarily directed towards a god or his cult. Furthermore, Garvie argues that it seems unlikely that 'two unconnected events which took place before the play began, and that have nothing to do with its action' are the key to Ajax's tragedy.[43] To be sure, Calchas' report goes some way towards explaining Athena's hostility to him, alongside the fact that she is Odysseus' champion and took his side in the Judgement of Arms (14; Homer *Odyssey* 11.547). But, for Garvie, the real purpose of the messenger's report of Calchas' speech is to re-establish, after Ajax's apparent change of heart at 646-92, our sense of pride in his heroic stature and thus to prepare us for his final speech.

Garvie's arguments certainly undermine any straightforward reading of *Ajax* as an exemplary dramatic lesson in the dangers of *hubris* towards the gods. And, as Fisher points out,

146

there is a real problem in seeing the punishment of *hubristai* as a defining feature of Greek tragedy anyway – if tragic heroes are too hubristic then they do not evoke the pity and unanswered questions about the justice of the world which (however much such expectation is the product of 'recasting') we *expect* from tragedy as a genre.[44] Athena's warning to Odysseus in the opening scene of the play and the tone and timing of the messenger's speech still make dramatic sense without recourse to *hubris* as an explanatory concept.

But there are, in my view, good reasons for keeping *hubris* and its several senses as a frame of reference for understanding this play's complex protagonist. And, despite his concern to undo the 'traditional' religious reading of *hubris*, not to mention a judicious reluctance to be pinned down on the exact extent of Ajax's *hubris*, Fisher seems to agree. For he concedes that the appropriate and yet upsetting quality of Ajax's suicide reflects a feeling that 'his *hubris* and other faults are almost as important as his heroic valour and nobility' and that 'more unalloyed sympathy is experienced rather for his dependants'.[45] But he points out that Ajax's reported boasts and rejection of Athena's aid is 'patently less offensive' than other verbal taunts issued against gods by humans in epic and tragedy: he is not in the same league as Salmoneus (a mythical king) and Capaneus (one of the 'Seven Against Thebes'), both of whom issued direct denials of Zeus's thunderbolt-based capabilities and challenged him to prove them wrong.[46] This is indicated by the fact that Athena did not punish the behaviour reported by Calchas immediately and, even after all Ajax's gross and violent offences, the anger that persists from these insults will pursue him only for one day. On this reading, Ajax is a *hubristês* after all: but his *hubris* is of a trivial order when compared to that of other mythical hot-heads.

Furthermore, there *is* evidence to suggest that *hubris* can be used to refer to acts of pride which bring the agent into the area of impious transgression beyond human limitations. The Chorus of Aeschylus' *Eumenides* say this in relation to lawless and tyrannical behaviour: 'the god grants power to moderation in every form, but he oversees other matters in different ways.

I have a timely word of advice: arrogance (*hubris*) is truly the child of impiety' (528-34). And then there is Darius in the *Persians*, who predicts that Xerxes' army will 'meet their crowning disaster in requital for their *hubris* and impious thoughts (*atheôn phronêmatôn*)' (808-9). He explains that the Persians, 'restrained by no religious awe' have destroyed Greek temples, altars and statues of gods. Darius also says that 'mortal man' should not vaunt himself excessively 'for *hubris*, when it has matured, ... reaps an abundant harvest of tears'. Darius warns against greed and the squandering of wealth: 'Zeus, in truth, is a chastiser of overweening pride and corrects with heavy hand.' He says that Xerxes 'has been warned to be prudent (*sôphronein*) by the voice of God' and that 'vaunting rashness' (*huperkompôi thrasei*) will draw divine punishment. These and other examples show an intimate connection between impious acts and excessive, boastful self-regard and *hubris*. They also show (*contra* Fisher) that such boastfulness and *hubris* can provoke divine retribution.

It is hard to escape the conclusion that Ajax's arrogant attitude towards Athena and the divine realm in general has garnered her disapproval. An Aeschylean character would call the Sophoclean Ajax impious and ripe for divine punishment – and he might associate him with *hubris*. An Athenian audience would probably do the same. But if Ajax is tainted with religious *hubris*, we need not conclude that his acts of self-assertion in relation to other mortals are tantamount to *hubris*. And even if they *can* be described as *hubris* (as they are by Menelaus), it does not follow that this is a negative aspect of the hero. As I hinted in the last chapter, Ajax and Teucer may both, and in their different ways, embody the kind of hubristic behaviour which, while transgressive in societal or legal terms, is sometimes necessary in the face of tyranny and injustice.

Ajax after Sophocles

The *Ajax's* staging of madness, humiliation and different models of masculinity in a battlefield context of same-side conflict has strong affinities with various narrative responses to war in the twentieth century. One thinks of the feuding sergeants (one brutal(ised), the other Messianic) in Oliver Stone's 1986 Vietnam movie, *Platoon*. There is the isolation from community and the loss of self masterfully depicted in *The Deer Hunter*. There is the loneliness, horror and insanity in one German soldier's experience of the Great War described so carefully and movingly in Remarque's 1929 novel *All Quiet On The Western Front*.

Perhaps the ubiquity of war in the news, in books and in film causes us to read a play like *Ajax* in the light of twentieth- and twenty-first-century images of its effects on minds, bodies and communities. We will even see that one modern version of our tragedy explicitly embraces and parades the play's 'relevance' to society and military policy in Reagan's America. It may also be the case that this and other Greek tragedies have left their mark on all kinds of imaginative writing about and depictions of war in those periods where Attic drama has been known and valued. But I will now turn to forms of influence and recasting which explicitly invoke Ajax or rewrite *Ajax*. Details and dates of many of the works of art which I consider to be significant examples in the post-Sophoclean 'reception' of our tragedy and Ajax's myth in general can be found in the Chronology on pp. 200-2 below. A proper study of the cultural impact and reception of our tragedy and its associated myths from the fifth century to the modern day needs a book to itself. Here I can only provide the briefest of surveys and a few tentative suggestions as to where, why and how Sophocles' hero has resurfaced in western culture.

Sophocles himself explored the aftermath of Ajax's death in two tragedies which are now lost, the *Teucer* and the *Eurysaces*. We have a fragment of the former tragedy in which Telamon laments the death of his son but no information for the content of the latter. There was also a *Teucer* by the Roman tragedian Pacuvius: Cicero quotes Telamon's angry reproaches to Teucer (*De Oratore* 2.46.193). The *Eurysaces* was also turned into Latin by Accius. On the basis of fragments from this version and a passage from Justin, Jebb conjectures that the Greek *Eurysaces* staged Teucer's return to the old Salamis from the new Salamis he had founded in exile on Cyprus.[47] Telamon is now dead, but Eurysaces does not allow Teucer to remain in Salamis and the bowman settles instead among the Gallaeci of Spain. These two tragedies and their Roman counterparts indicate that Ajax's suicide is held to have the same kind of far-reaching familial consequences as Oedipus' actions: these are more easily visible to us because of extant tragedies like *Seven Against Thebes, Antigone, Oedipus at Colonus* and *Phoenician Women*.

Sophocles was not the last Greek tragedian to treat Ajax's humiliation and downfall. In the fourth century, Astydamas wrote an *Ajax Mad* and Carcinus wrote an *Ajax* but we know nothing about them. Another *Ajax* by Theodectes seems to have drawn on Aeschylus' staging of the Judgement of Arms: Aristotle's *Rhetoric* refers to a speech in it by Odysseus which fits such a context (1400a27-9). This tragedy may also have drawn on a pair of surviving rhetorical prose speeches by the proto-Cynic philosopher Antisthenes who was a pupil of the prominent sophist Gorgias and a friend of Socrates. In the first of these speeches, Ajax makes the case for being the deserving recipient of Achilles' arms.[48] In the second speech, Odysseus argues that he is the worthier man for the prize. Both speeches are early examples of a tradition in which the Judgement of Arms became a regular topic around which Greek and Roman rhetoricians and their pupils could compose imaginary declamations which were persuasive and yet matched the characters and literary histories of the two heroes.

Antisthenes' speeches set up a contrast which will endure in the Roman declamatory and poetic traditions: there is Ajax as the man of great stature, open combat and deeds (*erga*) and Odysseus as the shifty, cunning and covert operative whose facility with words (*logoi*) can always trump his opponent's straight-talking mode. Odysseus the rhetorician can use speech to manipulate the judges' assessment of the two heroes' past actions in a manner which Ajax is able to anticipate but powerless to match. These contrasts are found in Sophocles and his poetic predecessors but the quasi-forensic prose format makes them starker. Antisthenes gains these contrasts by drawing on an Odysseus who is much more sinister, unprincipled and untrustworthy than the hero of Homer and *Ajax*. This is the Odysseus of the post-Homeric Epic cycle, Sophocles' *Philoctetes* and Euripides' *Hecuba*. In one sense, Antisthenes helps us to see the subtlety with which Ajax and Odysseus are presented in our play; we have seen how Ajax takes on 'Odyssean' insights and qualities while Odysseus' facility with *logoi* ultimately serves his respect for Ajax rather than hatred.

Antisthenes also shows an ironic and witty awareness of Ajax's fate as staged by Sophocles. Where Ajax's speech has rebuked Odysseus for the cowardice of his single-handed covert operations, Odysseus mocks Ajax for hiding behind his huge shield, and for 'toiling openly and in vain' with the help of others. He says that Ajax does not know how to fight, but attacks in anger like a wild boar: 'Some day you may kill your-self, falling on something' (2.6). It is as if Antisthenes' Odysseus 'knows' his Sophocles (and hence, the future). Ajax's speech invokes Sophocles in a less knowing way: in attacking Odysseus' fondness for secrecy, he proudly says 'I would not venture to do anything in secret' (1.5). These words jar with Ajax's night-time attack and suicide in our play: Ajax does *not* know his future self. Odysseus also has an awareness of the complicity between poetry and heroic fame, an awareness which recalls the treatment of Pindar which I discussed in Chapter 2. Odysseus hopes that any poet who is 'wise in matters of excel-lence (*aretê*)' will make him 'a man of much endurance, much intelligence, much contrivance, and a city-sacker, and will say that I alone captured Troy' (2.14). But this amusing awareness of his Homeric image (and the Pindaric condemnation of that image) is complicated by Odysseus' closing statement that this wise poet will liken Ajax's nature 'to that of sluggish mules and grazing cattle, who let others rope them and yoke them'. This reminds us of the animals whom Ajax has rounded up and slaughtered, and perhaps of the power which Athena exerts over him. But by invoking Sophocles' *Ajax*, this image also draws attention to its own inadequacy: Sophocles' 'wisdom' about 'excellence' has produced a hero whose problems and powers could never be fairly reduced to the degrading image which *this* Odysseus projects. Although Antisthenes wants to figure Odysseus as an emblem of military versatility, endurance, mental agility and rhetorical prowess, the complexity, pathos and grandeur of the Sophoclean Ajax still haunts the exchange.

Roman Republican tragedy took up Ajax's story, and while only fragments survive, the plays of Livius, Andronicus, Ennius, Pacuvius and Accius undoubtedly drew on Sophocles' tragedy and the Roman educational tradition in which the Judgement was a rhetorical *controversia* ('topic for debate'). But the most influential Roman writer to treat Ajax's dispute with Odysseus (Ulysses) and his subsequent death is Ovid (43 BC – AD 17). In book 13 of his hexameter poem, the *Metamorphoses*, Ovid's presentation of opposed speeches from the two heroes draws explicitly on the poet's training in *controversiae*.[49] Some of their arguments are reprised from Antisthenes, and again, Ulysses' eloquence (*facundia*) and cleverness are stressed. Ulysses contrasts his tactical intelligence with Ajax's brute force: the latter has 'strength without understanding (*ingenium*)' (13.363). Ovid tells us that the Greek chiefs' decision 'proved the power of *facundia* and the orator carried off the brave arms of the man' (13.382-3). Here, there is 'more than a hint of a celebration of the poet's own powers'.[50] Ajax and Ulysses offer two differing constructions of reality: Ovid seems to be asserting the '*priority* of words over deeds' and thus questioning an image of epic and historical tradition as a faithful mirror of 'things done'.[51]

This questioning aesthetic is not completely divorced from that of Greek tragedy. But Ovid's distinctive signatures of humour and his self-conscious critique of epic heroism are also on display. For example, Ulysses argues that Achilles' arms do not just need strength to carry them: they require a mind that can appreciate their beautiful divinely-wrought designs (13.290-5). Surely Thetis did not envisage Achilles' shield, 'a work of such art', clothing so 'rough and stupid' a soldier? Ulysses gives a brief set-piece description (*ecphrasis*) of some of the shield's relief-work depicting the world (a miniature version of *Iliad* 18.478-608). Having demonstrated his own appreciation of the shield (and hence, the world) he claims that Ajax asks for armour which he cannot understand (*non ... intellegit*). Here, Ajax's 'stupidity' is figured as aesthetic incapacity and ignorance of the cosmos – like Ovid himself, Ulysses scorns and deflates the traditional epic respect for heroic brawn. Perhaps Ovid does not want us to invoke the cosmic understanding which Ajax displays in Sophocles' deception speech but such an invocation highlights the manner in which Ajax's ethos is subject to very different representations and agendas in ancient literature.

The Ovidian Ajax has rhetorical power by virtue of being anti-rhetorical but his style betrays excessive vehemence and anger.[52] He commits suicide straight after the debate: the motifs of divine-sent madness and the attack on the cattle are not there. But the pathos, madness and anger of the Sophoclean Ajax still haunts Ovid's treatment. Ajax is 'unable to govern his anger' before he speaks, and when he is about to kill himself we are told that he 'could not withstand one passion; and resentment (*dolor*) conquered the unconquered hero' (13.3, 385-6). Ovid also seems to draw on our tragedy's use of Hector's sword as a significant object. As he seizes the sword to kill himself, Ajax shouts 'But this at least is mine; or does Ulysses claim this also for himself?' (13.387). This allusive line gives the Sophoclean motif a powerful twist: the sword is proof of Ajax's status as a match for Hector in battle. While Ulysses' words have won the day, Ajax's sword offers indisputable evidence of his great deeds. Perhaps Ovid concedes that tradition can assert the priority of certain 'realities' and 'deeds' over words after all.

Post-classical representations and uses of Ajax in art and literature were heavily influenced by Ovid's rendition. The most bizarre of these must be a prose discourse of 1576 by John Harington (godson to Elizabeth I). His *New Discourse of a Stale Subject Called the Metamorphosis of Ajax* is a Rabelaisian proposal for the introduction of a new type of toilet, complete with technical diagrams and levels of satire which led to a period of exile for the author. This mock encomium of a toilet deploys Ajax's name as the origin of the term 'a jakes' which meant both 'privy' and 'excrement' in the sixteenth century.

Harington says that when he lost the Judgement of Arms, Ajax became a 'perfit mal-content' who no longer sported the trappings of a gentleman. His description of Ajax's killing of the cattle is humorous and mocking. Here we have the first signs of an Ajax whose deluded slaughter provides material for comedy in the satirical heroic epics of Cervantes' *Don Quixote* (1604) and Samuel Butler's *Hudibras* (1663). In the former, Don Quixote mistakes a flock of sheep for two contending armies (I.III.iv). In the latter, a low-life butcher called Talgol has his trade elevated to epic status by comparison with Ajax *and* Don Quixote – Talgol has 'fought' more 'Troops' of sheep than either of them (I.II.309-10).

On the whole, though, the pathos and stature of the Sophoclean and Ovidian Ajax did not dissipate in post-classical representation. This is not the place to discuss (for example) the fascination with, and influence of, Ovid's *Metamorphoses* on English poetry in the seventeenth and eighteenth centuries.[53] But it should be noted that the famous version by John Dryden amplifies Ovid's subtle evocations of Sophocles' *Ajax*. Where Ovid has 'resentment conquered the unconquered hero', Dryden has 'Grief ... yields to Rage, to Madness, and Disdain'.[54] These additions effectively give the tragic and Sophoclean Ajax more prominence. In Ovid, the earth steeped in Ajax's blood produces a purple hyacinth whose petals contain a pattern which spells the letters AIAI. These letters are held by Ovid to refer to Ajax's name. But he says they also represent the lamentation of the boy Hyacinthus whose blood produces the same inscribed flower earlier in the poem (13.397-8; 10.162-219). But where Ovid states that the 'cry of woe' belongs to 'the boy' and the 'name' to 'the hero', Dryden's version omits these precise designations and renders the 'cry of woe' as 'Grief' – the same word which he has already used of Ajax's disastrous *dolor*. Thus, more explicitly than Ovid's original, Dryden allows the same connection between Ajax's name and the cry of grief which is made in Sophocles' play (430-1).

The vivid and violent manner of Ajax's death is depicted frequently on ancient Greek vases and relief sculpture both before and after Sophocles.[55] This great visual potential is

154

exploited in two late Renaissance frescoes by Giulio Romano and Giovanni Battista Castello. The first, executed by Giulio's assistants, forms part of his rather overbearing 'Mannerist' cycle of scenes associated with the Trojan war which decorated a room used as an armoury in the Palazzo Ducale in Mantua. It is striking that Giulio has Ajax impaled, not by a sword, but by a thunderbolt. As the naked and unarmed Ajax sprawls against a rock, Athena hovers with her shield and spear in the air and at a distance: she is not even looking at the transfixed hero with his open hands reaching helplessly to the heavens. As Hartt notes, this image is one of several in the room to depict Athena's triumph in the Trojan story and the terrors of disobeying or opposing her.[56] The thunderbolt connects Ajax's downfall with the goddess's displeasure much more directly than Sophocles does. But Giulio's transfixed hero is still a man whose lonely death we attribute to his own folly.

It would be surprising if Ajax did not also figure in the so-called Neo-Classical and Romantic visual art of the eighteenth and early nineteenth centuries. One of the most important European artists of this period, Henry Fuseli, used Sophocles' tragedy and Homer's Underworld episode to depict Ajax in a series of drawings and paintings.[57] One is entitled 'The Mad Ajax, after Slaying the Lambs, Recovers himself and Is Surprised by His Comrades'. Another has the 'The Mad Ajax, Turned toward His Son Eurysakes'. We also have a picture of Tecmessa and Eurysaces which was intended to form a larger painting of Ajax's suicide. It may be no accident that Fuseli was interested in visualising Ajax's madness. The late eighteenth and early nineteenth century was marked by an artistic back-lash against the notion of creative genius as a matter of sociability, order and decorum. As Craske points out, artists like Fuseli embodied 'the notion that artistic genius might be by definition a state of madness – a state of mind which placed a man outside the moral community and was feared more emphatically than death in the Enlightenment psyche'.[58] Craske shows how a self-portrait by Fuseli captures precisely this notion of 'mad genius'.

Such an aura of mania was directly fuelled by artists' respect for classical culture. It endowed the modern artist with a mystical quality which differentiated him from 'the typical man, the bourgeois, the philistine, and quite importantly the mere man of talent' and it established him as an heir of 'the ancient Greek poet and seer and like his classical counterpart, enabled him to claim some of the powers and privileges of the divinely possessed and inspired'.[59] But Fuseli's interest in Ajax may also reflect other themes which characterise his particular engagement with classical culture. Fuseli's drawings, writings and lectures evince a belief that 'the noble naiveté and sense of simple public spirit which was perceived to to have existed in Antiquity was largely unrecoverable'.[60] He admired the ancient world for its primal masculine energy – this nostalgia was probably derived from Winckelmann's hugely popular *Reflections on the Imitation of the Greeks* which Fuseli translated into English in 1765. His pessimistic view that ancient manhood could never be adequately regenerated by the modern artist or his culture suggests an allegorical interpretation for Fuseli's 'Ajax' pictures. For they betoken the death of an ancient and noble virility and the problematic relationship of the artist to sanity and community. They may even idealise heroic manhood as self-destructive.

Fuseli perhaps adds to such symbolism with his painting entitled 'In the Underworld, the Shade of Ajax Refuses a Reconciliation with Odysseus' which became an illustration in famous translations of Homer by both Pope and Cowper. This picture represents Ajax's ghost as physically perfect, but his eyes and demeanour are not quite human – Odysseus reaches to this demonic and angry figure in vain. However much the artistic culture which Fuseli was a part of (and yet hated) tried to resuscitate an ancient spirit of ideal manhood, and however much it attempted to reconcile the modern with the antique or to make old ruins and texts speak through new creations, the authentic nobility of the Greeks would remain as distant as Ajax's incommunicative and unforgiving ghost.

But how has Sophocles' *Ajax* fared as a tragedy for performance in the original, in translation or as an adaptation over the centuries? After antiquity, authentic Greek tragedy was never performed or translated before the 1500s and rarely performed in a fully public context in Europe before the 1880s.[61] But, as my chronology shows, several adaptations and translations of *Ajax* or the Judgement story were written and/or performed as drama or opera across Europe between 1582 and 1875. Shakespeare himself seemed to know something of the Sophoclean version (*Titus Andronicus* I.i.379-81).

The modern life of *Ajax* on the stage begins in 1882 when it was performed in the original as the first ever Cambridge Greek Play.[62] This tradition of putting on a Greek drama with student actors continues to this day. Photographs of the 1882 production show elaborate costuming and sets which reflect a burgeoning interest in the study of classical archaeology. We have already mentioned that Jebb considered the 'experiment' a success. But there is something about *Ajax* which has made it less popular for performance and adaptation beyond the confines of universities and schools in the twentieth century. Unlike the *Oresteia, Antigone, Oedipus Tyrannus*, or *Medea*, our tragedy has rarely found its way onto the professional stage and, as far as I am aware, never onto celluloid. It is hard to know why the play has been overlooked in this way. Perhaps Sophocles' Ajax disturbs modernity's classification of 'madness' and the 'pathological' as neatly opposed to 'rationality' and the 'normal'.[63] Perhaps it has become too difficult for us to acknowledge that Ajax's violent urges and extremism are traits which might characterise ourselves or else that we bear some responsibility for such traits when they are exhibited by others.

I want to conclude with two occasions when *Ajax* did make it to the modern stage. These two examples suggest that it *should* be a more popular choice for professional directors in the future. The first occasion is a performance of the tragedy in a community hall in an 'immigrant village' on the East Side of New York City in 1904.[64] This was put on by the local Greek community and, as Hartigan has shown, the play was an unexpected triumph. The *New York Daily Mirror* reviewed the show – a testament to the interest which Greek drama was generating at the time, because this paper normally concentrated on major productions in Manhattan, Boston and New Jersey. The anonymous reviewer found the production to be better than many of that season's metropolitan plays. The review indicates that the 'uptown contingent' were out in force to see the tragedy and that they were there 'because of curiosity'. They 'expected to be bored ... everyone knows that the *Ajax* is especially boring'. In patronising tones bordering on racism, the reviewer expresses amazement that 'a tragedy written twenty-four hundred years ago, enacted by amateurs drawn from the humble ranks of a small foreign colony ... riveted the attention and won enthusiastic plaudits of an intelligent and exacting assemblage'.[65]

It is unsurprising that the well-to-do of early twentieth-century New York had their aesthetic and social prejudices challenged by the *Ajax*. For the play is in many ways *about* the wrongness of prejudice: Ajax's vision is limited by narrow conceptions of 'nobility', and we have seen how the final scenes debunk the assumption that worth is bound up with birth and position. And where the reviewer thought that 'the pushcart industry' would not be up to 'a difficult style of dramatic art', (s)he missed the point that Greek tragedy's power in performance is not ultimately dependent on a perfect execution of its formal conventions and structures. This play about isolation from community and the shifting nature of identity was performed by Greeks in a new homeland which, as the reviewer's tone suggests, still regarded them as 'foreign'. It seems that themes which spoke very specifically to a Greek audience in the fifth century were now doing their work in a new context. Both as an expression of Greek heritage and culture *and* as a typically tragic interrogation of audience values, the community hall *Ajax* of 1904 showed that the play had an edgy political potential for modernity.

This potential was radically fulfilled over eighty years later in 1986 when a production of *Ajax* was staged in California and then moved to the American National Theatre in Washington DC. The script (in English) was adapted from Sophocles' original by Robert Auletta. He and director Peter Sellars gave the play a 'leftist' agenda. In a talk delivered three years later, Sellars makes this agenda clear: 'During this period, a very shocking event occurred. America bombed Libya, in an attempt, a sort of assassination attempt, I suppose. They tried to get Khaddafi, who for some reason was in another house that night. But there is the spectacle of this giant nation attempting to kill children, many miles away, because it was irritated. ... it was an event which made Reagan's imperial presidency complete.'[66] Sellars went on to explain his feeling that the American mass media and entertainment industries were stifling sophisticated political discussion and analysis in the USA. Echoing Noam Chomsky, he attributed this problem to media complicity with corporate and governmental interests. He turned to Sophocles because he saw a need 'to create an art that represents the public complexity, where one creates something that is, for example, as complex as the task of cleaning up a nuclear waste disposal site, which requires real thought, genuine expertise, and a series of very difficult decisions. It's not fun.' Refreshingly for a modern director, Sellars genuinely attempted to capture the complexity of Sophocles' hero and Greek drama's significance as a questioning civic form. He was anxious to confront audiences with what (he thought) they would normally turn away from: 'this disgusting debasement of what a human being truly is, what the genuine, heroic stature is of a human being'.

Drawing on the *Oresteia* and the facts of Athenian citizenship, Sellars idealised Greek tragedy as a 'survival mechanism about society, to teach people how to vote, to teach people what democracy is'. Thus he presented *Ajax* as a kind of ongoing trial where the Chorus functions as a jury to whom Ajax presents his case. But Athena is the final judge, so he is still lost. Auletta has Ajax commit an additional act of *hubris* against Athena: he rapes her. This violation represents 'more than just the violence of war; it is also sexist and racist (Athena is played by a black woman)'.[67] The play is set in an America which has 'just won a decisive victory in Latin America ... the war was a long and bloody one, marked, on the American side, by a great deal of bitterness, hostility and rivalry between factions of the armed forces'.[68] The Pentagon formed the backdrop to the play and Ajax first appeared in a transparent plastic box, wading in blood. When he stepped out of the box onto the stainless-steel

159

floor of the courtroom, the blood went everywhere, spattering across the stage with each gesture Ajax made. Sellars wanted to evoke an image of 'an abattoir ... stainless steel counters, where, after the butchery of the animals, they'd wash it all away, and there would be more butchery tomorrow'.[69] This graphic anti-militarism recalls Samuel Butler's brief comparison between Talgol and Ajax: Butler once redescribed military honour as 'Slaughter, and knocking on the head'.[70] When Sellars' Ajax lies dying on the beach, the blood is washed away by torrents of water pouring onto the stage: 'the whole rest of the play took place in the middle of this giant river'.[71] Ajax's own imagery of purification through death and (perhaps) Aristotelian notions of tragic catharsis are thus fused in a striking manner.

Ajax was played by the deaf actor Howie Seago. He used sign language to communicate his lines and these were interpreted by the Chorus. This device expressed Ajax's alienation and isolation. One is reminded of Knox's idea that the Sophoclean hero is 'deaf to appeals and persuasion'. Meanwhile, Odysseus was a 'CIA man' and the Atreids were sprucely-uniformed Pentagon generals. Tecmessa (Lauren Tom) was described as 'a Latin woman' and she 'testifies' with a microphone to the court that she is a captive from a country destroyed by the Americans. Athena describes Ajax as the 'force and heart of the American army'. His grandfather was a 'Sioux Chief' and he calls himself 'The Great American War Chief'. As McDonald puts it: 'not only does Ajax represent truth versus lies, he is the "true" American, in that he was descended from the original native people. The others came later and introduced their own rules.'[72] Meanwhile, Agamemnon's attacks on Ajax's and Teucer's birth and identity are transposed to an American context as he asserts his European ancestry: 'One doesn't become an American overnight, you know, just because one's father was an American general. My family has been here for well over two hundred years.' Agamemnon tells Ajax's supporters to 'forget your egos ... accept the democratic process'. But the democratic process in this play is manipulated by the lies, spin and corruption of the generals. Menelaus wants to spirit Ajax's body and memory away under a cloak of disinformation. Even Odysseus is now a self-seeking politician concerned only to win the war of information: he argues that Ajax cannot be 'disappeared' because he has too many friends and Agamemnon is 'running for major office'.

To many tastes, though not mine, the Auletta/Sellars *Ajax* must sound heavy-handed and unsubtle – a travesty, even, of Sophocles' original. Readers will be able to sense for themselves how this American version seems to have latched onto certain aspects of Sophocles' play while ignoring or simplifying others. But Sellars was actually following an established tradition of so-called 'interventionist' theatre. In this tradition, as Lorna Hardwick has recently shown very well, European socialist playwrights and directors such as Brecht and Piscator would often recast ancient drama and poetry with so-called 'alienation' and 'distancing' effects. Such effects included making direct comparisons between ancient characters and modern political figures or types in order to critique pre-war 'naturalist' theatre, capitalism and fascism.[73] The story of post-war 'interventionist' appropriations of Greek tragedy is fascinating and complicated – particularly in the work of Heiner Müller whose radical theatre in communist East Germany confounds any easy description of his classically-influenced work as political dissidence or pro-regime apology. His greatest contribution seems to have been to experiment so radically that his recastings of ancient material seemed subversive in terms of their form rather than their specific content.

The Auletta/Sellars production shows how a heavily ideological and 'interventionist' staging of *Ajax* can be spectacular and valuable as political art. But more might now be gained from staging *Ajax* in a manner which more overtly acknowledges the tragedy's strangeness, its resistance to definitive interpretation or judgement; the 'two-sidedness' of its characters and issues. To be sure, we would want to retain and transpose the fact that the play spoke directly to and questioned its audience's civic, moral and military values. I hope to have shown throughout this study that the lasting value of the *Ajax* can only be communicated if we recognise its refusal to simplify the problem of what constitute the proper limits of self-assertion, friendship, enmity, sanity, authority and one's obligations to family and community.

Notes

1. Playwright, Plot and Performance

1. On the fictionalising tendencies of ancient biographers see Lefkowitz, *Lives of the Greek Poets*.

2. Gould, 'Sophocles', p. 1423.

3. See Hall, 'Singing Actors', pp. 9-10. This last piece of evidence is derived from a marginal comment known as a 'scholion' (written by a 'scholiast') in a mediaeval manuscript of Aristophanes *Clouds* at line 1267. The comment mentions an actor called Tlepolemus 'who continually acted for Sophocles'. These comments (scholia) which accompany the transmitted texts of Greek drama are often derived from different scholars' commentaries and notes made from the Hellenistic period (336-31 BC) onwards. Collections of scholia were probably first compiled in late antiquity, and the process continued in the early centuries of Byzantium. For more information on scholia, see Reynolds and Wilson, *Scribes and Scholars*. Falkner, 'Scholars Versus Actors', has a good discussion of scholia on Greek drama. The unreliable and anonymous *Life of Sophocles* (6) says that Sophocles wrote his dramas with actors' characters in mind.

4. Goldhill, *Reading Greek Tragedy*, p. 155.

5. Schefold, 'Sophokles' Aias', goes for a date of around 460 because he believes the play inspired a datable Attic lekythos vase which depicts Ajax kneeling in prayer before he kills himself. For details of the vase see *LIMC* 1.329.105. For a good summary of the arguments and scholarship on the dating of the play see Garvie, *Ajax*, pp. 6-8.

6. See Robert, 'Sophocle, Périclès, Hérodote'.

7. For readings which bring *Ajax's* engagement with Athens' political or ideological structures and discourses to the fore in different ways see, for example, Goldhill, 'Great Dionysia'; Meier, *Political Art of Greek Tragedy*, pp. 167-87; Gasti, 'Sophocles' *Ajax*'; Rose, 'Historicizing Sophocles' *Ajax*'.

8. For sources and evidence on the City Dionysia, see Csapo and Slater, *Context of Ancient Drama*, pp. 103-65 and Pickard-Cambridge, *Dramatic Festivals*, pp. 58-104. For good analyses of how the festival instantiates Athens' status as a polis, democracy and imperial power see Goldhill, 'Great Dionysia'; Cartledge, ' "Deep Plays" '; Wilson, *Athenian Institution of the Khorêgia*.

9. For the details and importance of such conventions and settings see Taplin, *Greek Tragedy in Action*; Rehm, *Greek Tragic Theatre*; Wiles, *Tragedy in Athens*.

10. For a sense of the debate and a range of views see Easterling, 'A Show for Dionysus'; Friedrich, 'Everything to do with Dionysus?'; Seaford, 'Something to do with Dionysus'; Carpenter and Faraone, *Masks of Dionysus*; Sourvinou-Inwood, 'Something to do with Athens'.

11. See Wilson, *Athenian Institution of the Khorêgia*.

12. On these pre-play ceremonies see Goldhill, 'Great Dionysia'. On the unresolvable question of whether Athenian women were in the audience of Attic tragedy and comedy see Goldhill, 'Representing Democracy'.

13. Goldhill, 'Great Dionysia', p. 113.

2. Context and Tradition

1. For an excellent introduction to the uses and definition of Greek myth see Buxton, *Imaginary Greece*.

2. For the definition of myth conveyed in this paragraph see Martin, *Language of Heroes*, pp. 1-40; Gould, 'Myth, Memory and the Chorus'.

3. What on earth a 'tradition' is (and who decides what *counts* as 'traditional' or 'untraditional') is a highly problematic question, but even the most sceptical and iconoclastic of critics have found the notion of tradition difficult to dispense with entirely. See Martindale, *Redeeming the Text,* pp. 23-9.

4. For more details of the vases, probable dates and where they can be viewed, see Garvie, *Ajax*, pp. 3-4; March, 'Sophocles' *Ajax*'. A full catalogue and description of vases and other types of art depicting Ajax can be found at *LIMC* 1.1.314-36. Some of these are illustrated at *LIMC* 1.2.232-52. On some vases, Ajax throws himself, or prepares to throw himself, on his sword. On others, he stabs himself by hand. An Etruscan statuette (460 BC) depicts him stabbing himself in his left armpit. This reflected a version of Ajax's story according to which he was invulnerable except for his side or armpit.

5. We do not have a date for this trilogy. See Jebb, *Ajax*, pp. xix-xxiii and Garvie, *Ajax*, pp. 4-5, for discussion of what we can know about it from meagre fragments and ancient scholia to our play.

6. See the scholion to *Ajax* 815 (translated in Csapo and Slater, *Context of Ancient Drama*, p. 28).

7. On the difficulties of how the suicide was staged in our play see below, pp. 101-3 and bibliography cited there. Unlike Sophocles, Aeschylus seems to have followed the 'armpit' version.

8. Jebb, *Ajax*, pp. xxi-xxii.

9. Burian, 'Myth into *Muthos*', p. 193.

10. See Goldhill, *Reading Greek Tragedy*, pp. 33-56; Sommerstein,

Eumenides, pp. 13-32, 216-18; Rosenbloom, 'Myth, History and Hegemony', pp. 115-16.

11. See Hall, *Persians*, pp. 9-13; Harrison, *Emptiness of Asia*.

12. See Grégoire and Orgels, 'L'*Ajax* de Sophocle', for Ajax as Alcibiades; For Ajax as Cimon see Brown, 'Pindar, Sophocles'; Whitman, *Sophocles*; Evans, 'A Reading'. OKell, 'Themistocles' offers a neat set of correspondences between Ajax and historiographical representations of Themistocles.

13. On the problem with such 'political allegorising' see Goldhill, 'Modern Critical Approaches', p. 344. Sophocles' *Ajax* can be, and has been read 'allegorically' in a number of ways which make him a cipher for elite leadership in the Athenian democracy and empire. Rose, 'Historicising Sophocles' *Ajax*', sees him as a general who represents an endorsement of aristocratic paternalism and imperial hegemony. *Ajax* can also be fitted into the thesis of Griffith, 'Brilliant Dynasts', where tragedy's focus on aristocratic heroes before a mass festival-audience mediated between 'conflicting class interests and ideologies within the *polis*' to produce 'solidarity without consensus' (pp. 109-10). See Goldhill, 'Civic Ideology', for a critique of this view. Rosenbloom, 'Ponêros to Pharmakos', takes Griffiths' approach further and suggests that *Ajax* figures its hero and Odysseus as competing models of elite leadership whose behaviours nevertheless deconstruct civic drama's usual configurations of the new moneyed elite as morally bankrupt. See my own comments at pp. 124-30.

14. See Kearns, *Heroes of Attica*, p. 193.

15. Seaford, *Reciprocity and Ritual*, p. 113.

16. I think that Ajax's consecration as a hero is more of a main concern in *Ajax* than does Garvie, *Ajax*, p. 6. But that is not to say that the tragedy is just 'about' Ajax's cult-heroic status. Seaford, *Reciprocity and Ritual*, argues that hero-cult is crucial for understanding the function and shape of many surviving Attic tragedies, and I am indebted to this fine study throughout.

17. For stress on Salamis or Athens' link with it, see 134-5, 201-4, 596, 859-65, 1216-22. On the role of the Salaminioi in cult see Seaford, *Reciprocity and Ritual*, pp. 398-9. Seaford argues that the Chorus's duty to protect Eurysaces (565-77) and carry out Ajax's requests (685-6) prefigure this role.

18. This is pointed out by Belfiore, *Murder Among Friends*, p. 106.

19. This gloss on 'intertextuality' does not cover the full extent of the term's application and usage in modern critical discourse. For the nuances and a sense of why the coinage (of Julia Kristeva) is more than a mere synonym for 'influence', 'echo' or 'allusion', see Hinds, *Allusion and Intertext*. For accessible accounts of different forms of tragic intertextuality see Goldhill, *Reading Greek Tragedy*, pp. 247-9, and Burian, 'Myth into *Mythos*', pp. 193-8.

20. For succinct accounts of all the controversy surrounding the dating and nature of what J.M. Foley has aptly called the 'oral-derived' poetry of Homer, see the essays of Morris, Foley, Ford and Russo collected in I. Morris and B. Powell, *A New Companion to Homer*.

21. Garvie, *Ajax*, p. 1.

22. For an introduction to these other epics (lost after the fifth century save a few fragments and summaries), see Davies, *Epic Cycle*. It is not completely certain that all poems from the Epic Cycle post-date Homer. See Dowden, 'Homer's Sense of Text'.

23. The most famous and obvious example of a Sophoclean choral song with strong 'gnomic' qualities is the so-called 'Ode to Man' in Sophocles' *Antigone* 332-75. On this, see Segal, 'Sophocles' Praise of Man', and *Tragedy and Civilization*, pp. 152-7; Goldhill, *Reading Greek Tragedy*, pp. 203-5. Segal shows how this ode's praises of civilisation are ironically undercut by the rest of the play. Sophocles clearly liked to have his choruses' maxims undermined in this way.

24. See (e.g.) Homer *Iliad* 11.563, 591; 15.471, 560.

25. See my comments at pp. 113-18. See also Daly, *Horizontal Resonance*, and Rosenbloom, 'Ajax is *Megas*'.

26. Ajax is described as a *herkos Achaiôn* ('bulwark of the Greeks') at Homer *Iliad* 3.229, 6.5, 7.211 and elsewhere. The only other hero to be so-described is (of course) Achilles (1.284). See Worman, '*Herkos Achaiôn* Transformed', for an excellent analysis of the way in which Sophocles uses and tranforms this Iliadic image of Ajax's bulk and protective solidity in relation to a spatial schema of encirclement, entrapment, defence and extrusion.

27. For good comments on this, see Stanford, *Ajax*, p. 274.

28. Garvie, *Ajax*, p. 138.

29. Here, my emphasis is a little different from that of Davidson, 'The Parodos', p. 165. He sees the *parodos* as beginning a 'sympathetic reappraisal' of Ajax which 'counteracts' the image of the prologue.

30. Taplin, *Greek Tragedy in Action*, p. 108.

31. See, for example, Zanker, '*Ajax* and Heroic Values'.

32. See pp. 67-73.

33. For rhapsodic performance of Homer at the Panathenaea, see Lycurgus 1 [*Against Leocrates*] 102; Parke, *Festivals*, p. 34; Goldhill, *Poet's Voice*, pp. 167-73.

34. See Loraux, *Invention of Athens*.

35. For interplay between epic intertextuality and fifth-century context as crucial for understanding the play see studies as diverse as Goldhill, 'Great Dionysia'; Seaford, *Reciprocity and Ritual*; Gill, *Personality*; Rose, 'Historicising Sophocles' *Ajax*'; Evans, 'A Reading'; Sorum, '*Ajax* in Context'.

36. See, for example, Griffin, 'Social Function' and 'Sophokles and the Democratic City'.

37. For Ajax's appeal to Achilles in Homer, see *Iliad* 9.623-55. On Tecmessa and Ajax, see pp. 63-73.

38. See pp. 140-1.

39. On the ambiguity of the sword and intertextuality between 485-582 and *Iliad* 6, see pp. 67-73, 78-80.

40. Here I adopt a reconstruction of Alcaeus fragment 112 line 10 found in a scholion to Sophocles *Oedipus Tyrannus* 56. Another scholion (Aeschylus *Persians* 352) has a slightly different version: 'men are a city's warlike tower'.

41. That Sophocles knew the specific line is made even more likely when we look at *Oedipus Tyrannus* 56-7: '... a tower (*purgos*) or ship is nothing without men who live inside it'.

42. See Aeschylus *Persians* 349, Herodotus 8.61.2 and the comments of Harrison, *Emptiness of Asia*, p. 71.

43. See Bowra, *Greek Lyric Poetry*, pp. 379-80 for a speculative reading of these couplets as Pisistratid propaganda.

44. Aristophanes *Lysistrata* 1236-8; Theopompus fragment 65 K-A; Antiphanes fragment 85 K-A.

45. For detailed readings of Pindar's treatment of Ajax's story see Most, *Measures of* Praise, pp. 148-82; Walsh, *Varieties of Enchantment*, pp. 37-61; Nisetich, *Pindar and Homer*, pp. 1-23; Pratt, *Lying and Poetry*, pp. 121-8.

46. See Garvie, *Ajax*, pp. 4-5. *Nemean* 7 could be 480s or 460s. *Nemean* 8 could be 460s or 450s. *Isthmian* 4 could be 479/8 BC.

47. Like Garvie, *Ajax*, p. 4, I think that 'secret votes' refers to cheating rather than a secret ballot. Brown, 'Pindar, Sophocles', argues that *Ajax* is a direct response to *Nemean* 8 which he dates to 445 and argues that both works concern the Thirty Years Peace.

3. Setting the Scene

1. The most important study of 'implied' action in tragic speech is Taplin, *Greek Tragedy in Action*. See also Seale, *Vision and Stagecraft*. 'Implied' action and scene-setting in tragic characters' speeches is similar to techniques employed in radio drama. Even with the use of sound effects, radio plays and soaps often require a character to subtly set the scene in as natural and unobtrusive a way as possible.

2. Where Dutta, *Ajax*, translates *skênais* as 'tent', Garvie, *Ajax*, pp. 124-5 insists on 'huts' on the grounds that a building seems to be implied at 63-5 and that the word used by Athena is the same as the word (*skênê*) which was commonly used to refer to the actual stage building that would have formed the backdrop in the theatre of Dionysus. It is impossible to know for sure what an audience would have imagined when Athena refers to Ajax's dwelling as *skênai*. Dobrov, *Figures of Play*, pp. 61-2, makes much of it as a 'metatheatrical' reference to the stage-building.

3. See Bowie, 'End of Sophocles' *Ajax*', p. 114.

4. See Segal, *Tragedy and Civilization,* p. 112 and Holt, 'Ajax's Ailment', p. 26.

5. Sorum, '*Ajax* in Context', p. 362. See also Knox, *Word and Action,* pp. 144-7; Whitman, *Sophocles,* p. 73; Zanker, '*Ajax* and Heroic Values'; Winnington-Ingram, *Sophocles: an Interpretation,* p. 60.

6. Taplin, *Greek Tragedy in Action,* p. 40.

7. There may be further irony here. Ajax chooses to kill the imaginary Odysseus with a whip (110). This is a fitting instrument given stories of Odysseus' use of a whip against himself in order to perfect his disguise as a beggar or slave before entering Troy on a spying mission. See Antisthenes' *Odysseus* (2.10 in Gagarin and Woodruff, *Early Greek Political Thought*).

8. See Garvie, *Ajax,* p. 123; Blundell, *Helping Friends.*

9. For a good sense of the debate and the issues see Taplin, *Greek Tragedy in Action,* p. 185 n. 12; Heath, *Poetics of Greek Tragedy,* pp. 165-6; Garvie, *Ajax,* p. 124.

10. Goldhill, *Reading Greek Tragedy,* p. 183.

11. This contrast through repetition is noticed and described cautiously as 'probably intended' by Stanford, *Ajax,* p. 270. Segal, *Tragedy and Civilization,* pp. 109-51 also (to some extent) relies on the recognition of significant repetitions in the play.

12. Garvie, *Ajax,* p. 124.

13. See Abel, *Metatheatre*; Hubert, *Metatheater*; Segal, *Dionysiac Poetics.*

14. See Seale *Vision and Stagecraft,* pp. 144-76; Davis, 'Politics and Madness', pp. 146-7; Falkner, 'Making a Spectacle'; Pucci, 'Gods' Intervention'; Segal, *Sophocles' Tragic World,* pp. 16-25; Dobrov, *Figures of Play,* pp. 57-69.

15. Dobrov, *Figures of Play,* p. 65.

16. Dobrov, *Figures of Play,* pp. 64-5.

17. Falkner, 'Making a Spectacle', p. 38.

18. Falkner, 'Making a Spectacle', p. 38.

19. Dobrov, *Figures of Play,* p. 24. For a good sense of what is at issue see Taplin, 'Comedy and the Tragic'; Dobrov, *Figures of Play,* pp. 1-53.

20. See Garvie, *Ajax,* p. 138: 'It is no accident that four times (154, 156, 160-1, 169) it [i.e. the Chorus] describes him as *megas,* "great".'

21. Winnington-Ingram, *Sophocles: an Interpretation,* p. 22 n. 35 counts thirty-six occurrences of the word *megas.* It is particularly prevalent in the *parodos* with nine appearances. On this, see also Knox, *Word and Action,* p. 144; Davidson, 'Parodos', p. 175 n. 12.

22. Here, I differ from the interpretation of Rose, 'Historicizing Sophocles' *Ajax*', p. 70 who misses the reciprocity and posited interdependence between 'big' and 'little' people in lines 154-66. It is true that the Chorus validate a 'fundamentally hierarchical view of society' but it is also important to note that the idea of *interdependence* between 'big' and 'little' is part of the Chorus's view of their relationship with Ajax and that this is not simply hierarchical or paternalistic.

23. Rose, 'Historicizing Sophocles' *Ajax*', p. 71.

24. Gould, 'Collective Experience', and Goldhill, 'Collectivity and Otherness', give a good sense of the difficulties of interpreting the role of tragic choruses in relation to the Athenian audience.

25. Rose, 'Historicizing Sophocles' *Ajax*', p. 70.

26. These are the views of Rose, 'Historicizing Sophocles' *Ajax*', pp. 70-1, and Gardiner, *Sophoclean Chorus*, pp. 74-8, respectively.

4. Ajax and Tecmessa

1. For the vase, see *LIMC* 1.1.332.140 or Taplin, *Greek Tragedy in Action*, plate 11.

2. See Foley, *Female Acts*, pp. 90-2. For Tecmessa as a slave see Synodinou, 'Tecmessa in the *Ajax*'. For Tecmessa appropriating a wifely role she does not possess (via the echoes of Andromache) and then consolidating it after Ajax's death, see Ormand, 'Silent by Convention?', and his *Exchange and the Maiden*, p. 116.

3. Foley, *Female Acts*, p. 90.

4. Foley, *Female Acts*, pp. 91-2. Compare fragment 545 of Euripides' *Oedipus* (*TGrF* IV): 'the modest wife is the slave of her husband, the immodest wife in her folly despises her consort.'

5. Foley, *Female Acts*, p. 104.

6. On the role of concubines in Athens see [Demosthenes] 59.122 and the remarks of Foley, *Female Acts*, pp. 89-90. On the wisdom of keeping wife and concubine in different places see Lysias' conduct in section 22 of the same speech. For the evidence, bibliography, issues and controversy surrounding wives, inheritance and legitimacy in Athens, see Foley, *Female Acts*, pp. 67-79, 87-90.

7. For the divisive economic and social influence of a wife and her natal family and the problem of keeping both a slave concubine and a wife under one roof, see Euripides' *Andromache* with McClure, *Spoken Like a Woman*, pp. 158-204. See also Allan, *Andromache*; Foley, *Female Acts*, pp. 97-105.

8. Here, and in the next two sentences, I am indebted to the analysis of Knox, *Heroic Temper*, p. 42.

9. For the paradox that it is better to be happily mad than unhappily sane, see Euripides *Bacchae* 1260-3. Euripides' Phaedra rejects this view at *Hippolytus* 247-9.

10. Stanford, *Ajax*, p. 97.

11. Ajax's sentiment is echoed by later writers: see Aristotle *Politics* 1260a30-1; Democritus fragment 274 D-K. See also Dover, *Greek Popular Morality*, pp. 95-102.

12. McClure, *Spoken like a Woman*, p. 20.

13. Gill, *Personality*, p. 211.

14. See below, p. 77. The fact that Ajax describes himself as feminised, the fact that his suicide is not (we will soon see) completely manly and the fact that Tecmessa will speak up forcefully (despite Ajax's claim that silence is womanly) all hint at the kind of crisis and blurring of gender roles which seem to mark tragedy's treatment of women as objects of exchange. On such patterns in other tragedies, see Wohl, *Intimate Commerce*.

15. There is some ambiguity with 317-22 as to whether Tecmessa is saying (a) that Ajax moved from initially uncharacteristic womanly cries to deeper bull-like cries, or (b) that his shrill cries contrast with the bull-like bellowing of his more characteristic self. Garvie, *Ajax*, p. 155 reads the text in line with (b). Segal, *Tragedy and Civilization*, p. 134 seems to go for (a). Dutta's translation is ambiguous between (a) and (b). I am following (b) as more likely.

16. Segal, *Tragedy and Civilization*, p. 134.

17. These last two sentences, and the next two, are indebted to Segal, *Tragedy and Civilization*, p. 134.

18. The quotes are from Segal, *Tragedy and Civilization*, pp. 133-5.

19. On this device see Taplin, *Greek Tragedy in Action*, pp. 11-12. For ancient evidence and sources see Csapo and Slater, *Context of Ancient Theatre*, pp. 61, 258, 261f., 270-2.

20. Taplin, *Greek Tragedy in Action*, p. 108.

21. See pp. 136-41.

22. See Stanford, 'Light and Darkness Imagery', p. 180.

23. Winnington-Ingram, *Sophocles: an Interpretation*, p. 15.

24. Garvie, *Ajax*, p. 164.

25. Rose, 'Historicizing Sophocles' *Ajax*', p. 83. See also the arguments of Heath *Poetics of Greek Tragedy*, p. 179 n. 27, and Whitman, *Homer and the Heroic Tradition*, pp. 169-74.

26. Winnington-Ingram, *Sophocles: an Interpretation*, p. 14.

27. Gill, *Personality*, p. 206.

28. Garvie, *Ajax*, p. 185. See also Euripides *Bacchae* 367 and 508 where Pentheus' name is related to *penthos*, meaning 'suffering' or 'grief'. Etymology was a subject for theorising in the sophistic and philosophical circles which emerged in Athens in the latter part of the fifth century (see Plato *Cratylus* 435d).

29. The 'eagle' etymology is at Pindar *Isthmian* 6.53. A fourth-century Etruscan stamnos vase depicts Ajax about to commit suicide with a plant at his feet – its stem has *Aivas* written on it. This probably connects Ajax to the supposed marking AI on the petals of the *hyacinthus* flower. This connection is first attested in literature in the third century BC (Euphorion fragment 40). See p. 154 for Ovid's use of the connection.

30. Gill, *Personality*, p. 207. See also Williams, *Shame and*

Necessity, pp. 84-5 and Cairns, *Aidôs*, p. 231. Gill sees this 'internalised other' working to provoke shame in Homeric heroes too (e.g. Polydamas for Hector in *Iliad* 22).

31. See Strauss, *Fathers and Sons*; Griffith, 'King and Eye'.

32. For other versions of this anguished question from Sophoclean heroes, see *Antigone* 1099; *Philoctetes* 908, 970, 1350.

33. Gill, *Personality*, p. 207.

34. Garvie, *Ajax*, p. 169. See also Winnington-Ingram, *Sophocles: an Interpretation*, pp. 19, 29-30; Easterling, 'Tragic Homer'; Blundell, *Helping Friends*, pp. 74-7; Cairns, *Aidôs*, pp. 231-4; Heath, *Poetics of Greek Tragedy*, pp. 181-2.

35. On the value of maxims see Aristotle's *Rhetoric* 1394a20-1395b15.

36. This is pointed out by Easterling, 'Tragic Homer', p. 3.

37. For the condition of aged parents with no children to look after them, see also *Iliad* 24.386-92 and Hesiod *Theogony* 603-7. One might object that a two-word repetition from Homer in Tecmessa's speech could not activate recollection of the particular passage in book 5, especially when the formula (*gêrai lugrôi*) occurs several times (e.g. *Iliad* 10.79, 18.434, 23.644). In this particular case, the commentary-writers are silent or slightly coy: Stanford (*Ajax*, p. 123) calls it a 'variation' of *Iliad* 5.153 while Garvie (*Ajax*, p. 172) speaks of a parallel rather than specific allusion. At the very least, Tecmessa's use of a stock epic phrase conjures up more generally the Homeric and lyric commonplace of old age being hard (especially when the parents outlive their children).

38. See Jebb, *Ajax*, p. 83. Jebb points out that technical and prosaic words do find their way into Attic poetry, citing *euthunos* and *praktôr* at Sophocles *Electra* 953.

39. On different forms of *charis* and reciprocity, see Blundell, *Helping Friends*, pp. 32-7. The term is invoked throughout the play: see lines 12, 176, 1267, 1354, 1371.

40. Stanford, *Ajax*, pp. 269-70 and 301 offer the following examples of repetition in *Ajax*: 233, 359, 396-7, 854, 1205-6. But there are many more. Garvie's translation commendably preserves such repetitions in most cases, e.g. *ômoi. keithen keithen … êluthe* ('Alas! So it was from there, from there … that he came': 233). This repetition conveys Tecmessa's emotional state. But it also shows that Ajax really *has* come from the scene of the crime and really *has* done the deed – facts which the Chorus are finding it hard to face up to (221-32). The *Ajax* also contains significant repetitions which have longer intervals between them: see Stanford's 'index to selected topics' for references.

41. Stanford, *Ajax*, p. 270. Again, there is lots of *polyptoton* in *Ajax*. See, for example: 265-7, 362-3, 466-8, 522, 619-20, 839, 866, 923-5, 1133-4, 1283-7, 1389-92.

42. Ajax's jingle '*monos monois*' also contrasts with another of

Tecmessa's *polyptota* from earlier in the play: see '*koinos en konoisi*' (265) which stresses the option of Ajax sharing pain in common with Tecmessa and the Chorus.

43. Holt, 'Debate Scenes', p. 279.

44. See Adkins, *Merit and Responsibility*, p. 44, and Garvie, *Ajax*, p. 169.

45. Blundell, *Helping Friends*, p. 86.

46. Cairns, *Aidôs*, p. 223.

47. For details of this enhancement, see Easterling, 'Tragic Homer'. My analysis follows Easterling's closely.

48. Garvie, *Ajax*, p. 171.

49. As Garvie points out (*Ajax*, p. 172), Sophocles does not 'overdo the pathos' by making Ajax the killer of her father (or for that matter, her mother, who like Andromache's, has died of natural causes). There was a much later tradition that Ajax had killed Tecmessa's father (see Dictys Cretensis *Trojan War* 2.18). But Sophocles' wording clearly implies that he had nothing to do with his death in this version.

50. Goldhill, 'Great Dionysia', p. 117.

51. See p. 53 above and Goldhill, *Reading Greek Tragedy*, p. 197.

52. Taplin, *Greek Tragedy in Action*, p. 64, is right to say that the text yields no answer either way. Seale, *Vision and Stagecraft*, p. 157, and Heath, *Poetics in Greek Tragedy*, p. 183, complain that Ajax cannot have the shield throughout and that Eurysaces must be too young to carry it.

53. On our play's engagement with notions of dissent see Barker, 'Fall-out from Dissent'.

54. See Taplin, *Greek Tragedy in Action*, p. 64; Scullion, *Three Studies*, p. 93; Garvie, *Ajax*, p. 180.

55. For the side-door theory see Jebb, *Ajax*, p. 96; Stanford, *Ajax*, p. 136. Winnington-Ingram, *Sophocles: an Interpretation*, p. 32, argues that Tecmessa stays on stage. Heath, *Poetics of Greek Tragedy*, p. 184 has her collapsing 'distraught' on stage.

56. For the third *stasimon*, see below pp. 119-20.

5. Deception and Suicide

1. Gellie, *Sophocles: a Reading*, p. 12.

2. Sophoclean characters often announce their intention to deceive. See Sophocles *Electra* 35-77, *Philoctetes* 55-134, *Oedipus at Colonus* 399f. and 728f. But Blundell, *Helping Friends*, p. 83, points to Lichas' deception in *Trachiniae* as a parallel for Ajax's speech because in that case the lie is not explicitly trailed.

3. Knox, *Word and Action*, p. 135.

4. See Knox, *Word and Action*, pp. 134-40; Sicherl, 'Tragic Issue', p. 92.

5. Several classical Athenian texts indicate that palliative lying was seen as justified in Athenian popular morality. See Hesk, *Deception and Democracy*, pp. 151-79.

6. Segal, *Tragedy and Civilization*, p. 124. One problem with this view is that it may require us to think of a night-time attack as the *preserve* of Odysseus. But Odysseus is accompanied by Diomedes in the nocturnal operation of *Iliad* 10. While Odysseus is clearly a master of stealth-warfare in Homer, there is nothing to suggest that other heroes cannot honourably take part in such operations. Homer's Ajax is not a stranger to the deployment of cunning intelligence: see Bradshaw, 'The Ajax Myth', pp. 106-15.

7. This is the view of Garvie, *Ajax*, p. 129.

8. Taplin, *Greek Tragedy in Action*, p. 128.

9. Having said this, I do not deny the parallels between the deception speech and Sophocles' *Oedipus at Colonus* 609-10 and 624-8 as discussed by Seaford, *Reciprocity and Ritual*, pp. 135-6.

10. In this chapter I will use Garvie's prose translation because of its virtues of accuracy and clarity. But readers are encouraged to cross-reference to different verse translations in order to appreciate some of the *poetic* power of the deception speech.

11. See *Trachiniae* 129-35; *Oedipus Tyrannus* 1213; *Philoctetes* 305-6; *Oedipus at Colonus* 607-23.

12. Ajax's generalisation that nothing is beyond expectation (*aelpton*) recalls a fragment of the archaic iambic poet Archilochus (122.1).

13. As Cohen, 'Imagery', p. 30, points out, Ajax's description of himself as like iron dipped in water recalls the sword imagery in the play's early scenes (95, 219)

14. Ajax being genuine: Garvie, *Ajax*, p. 197; Gill, *Personality*, p. 211; Foley, *Female Acts*, p. 91. Ajax being insincere: Blundell, *Helping Friends*, p. 82 n. 104; Cairns, *Aidôs*, p. 234 n. 63.

15. Cohen, 'Imagery', p. 30.

16. Cohen, 'Imagery', p. 30.

17. Cohen, 'Imagery', p. 31.

18. It is difficult to tell how far Ajax is envisaging an expiation of 'religious' pollution incurred through the killing of the herdsmen or is merely referring to a washing off of the blood of the slaughtered animals. Sicherl, 'Tragic Issue', pp. 95-6 sees Ajax's wish to 'escape' Athena's anger as atonement while Garvie, *Ajax*, p. 188, rejects any idea that Ajax's death is intended as divine reconciliation or atonement.

19. For the deception speech's pervasive ambiguities, see, for example, Ferguson, 'Ambiguity in *Ajax*', and Goldhill, *Reading Greek Tragedy*, pp. 189-92. Goldhill points out that line 654 contains ambiguous syntax: the connective word which Garvie translates as 'well' is *alla*. This can indicate an adversative force, 'as if the structure of the rhetoric were "I pity her but none the less I'm going ..." '. But the connective can also convey a positive encouragement, to give the sense 'I pity her, and so I'll go, then ...'.

20. See Stanford, *Ajax*, p. 277; Cohen, 'Imagery'; Seaford, *Reciprocity and Ritual*, pp. 392-3.

21. The Greek is very poetic and rhetorical: *'echthrôn adôra dôra kouk onêsima'*. As Garvie, *Ajax*, p. 189 notes, this a 'common type of poetic expression, in which the noun is qualified by a cognate alpha-privative adjective' and 'either a negating or a pejorative sense is often possible'. The sentiment is also found in Euripides' *Medea* (618) and Aristophanes' *Wasps* (1160).

22. Here, I follow Seaford, *Reciprocity and Ritual*, p. 393, in seeing *toigar* ('therefore', 667) as expressing a direct connection with the preceding line about hostile gifts: '... the connection consists in the basic instability, embodied in the gift of the sword, of relations of amity and hostility. An enemy, Ajax says a little later (678-82), may become a friend, and a friend an enemy'. Heath, *Poetics of Greek Tragedy*, p. 187, thinks the connective takes us back to the reconciliation he seeks with Athena and his human enemies (656-7).

23. The inversion was first noted by the scholiast on this line. See also Winnington-Ingram, *Sophocles: an Interpretation*, p. 49. Heath, *Poetics of Greek Tragedy*, p. 187; Knox, *Word and Action,* p. 157; Gill, *Personality*, pp. 211-12. Moore, 'Dissembling Speech', p. 47, and Sicherl, 'Tragic Issue', pp. 80-1, want to make the lines sincere.

24. Gill, *Personality*, p. 212.

25. This is pointed out by Garvie, *Ajax*, p. 189.

26. Goldhill, *Reading Greek Tragedy*, pp. 190-1.

27. The quotation and the argument are from Gill, *Personality*, p. 211.

28. Vlastos, 'Equality and Justice', p. 172.

29. See Diller, *Gottheit und Mensch*, pp. 5-6.

30. See Gill, *Personality*, p. 212. Ajax uses a generalising plural (*hêmeis*: 'we') but is clearly referring primarily to himself. Why does he use a plural at all? Stanford, *Ajax*, p. 148 suggests that he almost means 'we mortals'.

31. Winnington-Ingram, *Sophocles: an Interpretation*, p. 47.

32. See Theognis 113-14 where the poet advises that the friendship of an evil man is like a poor harbour. Kamerbeek, *Ajax*, p. 144 suggests that Ajax is hinting at death as a solution to the treacheries of *philia*.

33. Knox, *Word and Action*, p. 141.

34. Blundell, *Helping Friends*, pp. 82-4, adduces the following parallels between Ajax's language in the deception speech and that of Tecmessa, Odysseus and the Chorus (along with contrasts between the professed 'yielding' of the speech and Ajax's character and language elsewhere): alteration of the mind with time (648f.; 594f., 1361), pity (652; 121, 510, 525, 580), softening under friends' influence (650-2; 330, 594f., 1353), yielding to the gods (655f., 666f.; 112f., 589f., 766-75).

35. Gill, *Personality*, p. 213. Although Gill does side with Ajax here, he also admits that 'it would be an over-simplification to suggest that the play validates totally Ajax's ethical attitude, or the problematic acts which derive from this'.

36. Winnington-Ingram, *Sophocles: an Interpretation*, pp. 64-6. Or, as Taplin, 'Yielding to Forethought', p. 127 puts it: 'this is insight without compromise, humanity without weakness'.

37. Seaford, *Reciprocity and Ritual*, p. 395.

38. Seaford, *Reciprocity and Ritual*, pp. 227-38. For the details of the parallels between mystic inscriptions and the fragments of Heraclitus see also Seaford, 'Immortality', pp. 14-22.

39. Seaford, *Reciprocity and Ritual*, p. 397.

40. Seaford, *Reciprocity and Ritual*, p. 399.

41. Seaford, *Reciprocity and Ritual*, p. 136.

42. More recently, Seaford has overtly and impressively defended his own brand of political reading. See Seaford, 'Social Function'.

43. Stanford, *Ajax*, p. 182.

44. Here, I am following the argument of Belfiore, *Murder Among Friends*, pp. 111-16.

45. Belfiore, *Murder Among Friends*, p. 116.

46. Belfiore, *Murder Among Friends*, p. 112

47. I say 'seems to' because there is some debate as to how far the noun *philos* is used to designate kin in the classical period. See Konstan, *Friendship in the Classical World*, p. 53. For counter-argument, see Belfiore, *Murder Among Friends*, pp. 19-20.

48. Goldhill, *Reading Greek Tragedy*, p. 81. Konstan, 'Greek Friendship', p. 89, argues against the majority view that *philia* entails 'objective' obligations. For him the term 'refers to friendly actions or treatment, whether of friends who behave attentively or of kin whose feelings and conduct are appropriately warm or loyal'.

49. Goldhill, *Reading Greek Tragedy*, p. 83.

50. Garvie, *Ajax*, p.193, points out that *erai* also implies a passionate desire for death at Sophocles *Antigone* 220.

51. Evans, 'A Reading', p. 77.

52. Garvie, *Ajax*, p. 192. See also Sicherl, 'Tragic Issue', p. 84.

53. See Wigodsky, 'The "Salvation" of Ajax'.

54. See Moore, 'The Dissembling Speech'.

55. Segal, *Tragedy and Civilization*, p. 114. See also Ferguson, 'Ambiguity in *Ajax*', for whom 'ambiguity is the theme of the play' (30).

56. Segal, *Tragedy and Civilization*, p. 114.

57. Goldhill, *Reading Greek Tragedy*, p. 190.

58. Goldhill, *Reading Greek Tragedy*, p. 192.

59. As stressed by Gill, *Personality*, pp. 213-16.

60. See above, p. 45. See Montmarquet, 'Epistemic Virtue', for philosophical accounts of epistemic virtue.

61. See Nussbaum, *Fragility of Goodness*, and Williams, *Shame and Necessity*.

62. For various accounts which seek to diminish the importance of Calchas' explanation see Reinhardt, *Sophocles*, pp. 29-30; Rosenmeyer, *Masks of Tragedy*, pp. 182-4; Garvie, *Ajax*, pp. 195-7.

63. We cannot be certain that there is a scene change here. Scullion, *Three Studies*, suggests that Ajax hides behind bushes when he exits at 692 and then returns to the area outside his tent once the Chorus and Tecmessa have gone off to look for him by the seashore. See Garvie, *Ajax*, p. 204 for obvious objections to this.

64. Segal, *Tragedy and Civilization*, p. 139.

65. Belfiore, *Murder Among Friends*, p. 107.

66. Loraux, *Tragic Ways*, p. 9.

67. See Belfiore, *Murder Among Friends*, pp. 106-7, for discussion and references.

68. After the battle of Plataea the Spartan warrior Aristodemus is deprived of posthumous glory because he had sought death too openly and to wipe out previous disgrace (Herodotus 9.71). Plato thinks that suicide should be punished with anonymous burial on the edge of a city because of its 'total lack of manliness' (*Laws* 9.873c-d).

69. See Homer *Odyssey* 10.53; *Iliad* 18.32-4.

70. Loraux, *Tragic Ways*, p. 54.

71. Loraux, *Tragic Ways*, p. 22.

72. Burnett, *Revenge*, p. 92.

73. Burnett, *Revenge*, p. 93.

74. Burnett, *Revenge*, p. 93.

75. Garvie, *Ajax*, p. 203.

76. Garvie, *Ajax*, p. 203. See also Taplin, *Greek Tragedy in Action*, p. 188, who thinks that the covering of the corpse is in some way connected with the replacement of the actor.

77. See Hesychius under *suspaston* and *andrometon*; Achilles Tatius *Leucippe and Clitophon* 3.20.7, 21.4.

78. For various solutions involving the *ekkuklema* see Webster, *Greek Theatre Production*, pp. 17-18 and Stanford, *Ajax*, pp. 173-4.

79. See Taplin, *Stagecraft of Aeschylus*, p. 443.

80. Heath, *Poetics of Greek Tragedy*, pp. 192-4.

81. Brušák, 'Signs in the Chinese Theatre', p. 63.

6. The Quarrel

1. Jebb, *Ajax*, p. xlv.

2. Here I agree with Malcolm Heath, one of the few critics to see Teucer in a favourable light. See Heath, *Poetics of Greek Tragedy*, pp. 198-205.

3. Winnington-Ingram, *Sophocles: an Interpretation*, p. 1, calls Teucer an 'Ajax-substitute – and a poor one … his inadequacy is pathetic'. Stanford, *Ajax*, pp. xlv-clvi, thinks he and Menelaus are like 'angry schoolboys' and accuses him of stooping to tactics which Ajax would never have contemplated. Garvie, *Ajax*, p. 216, thinks him 'mediocre'. For more Teucer-bashing, see Bowra, *Sophoclean Tragedy*, p. 38; Torrance, 'Sophocles', p. 279; Gellie, *Sophocles: a Reading*, pp. 22-3.

4. The quotation is from Goldhill, *Reading Greek Tragedy*, p. 195.

5. For the problematic status of bastards (*nothoi*) in classical Athens, see Ogden, *Greek Bastardy*. On the chauvinistic attitude of fifth-century Greeks towards non-Greeks, and of Athenian citizens towards aliens, see Cartledge, *Greeks*, pp. 36-62, 90-117; Harrison, *Greeks and Barbarians*. On tragedy's engagement with ideas of the barbarian 'other', see Hall, *Inventing the Barbarian*.

6. On the centrality of the hoplite ethic in classical Athens, see Vidal-Naquet, *Black Hunter*, pp. 85-9; Loraux, *Invention of Athens*, pp. 155-71; Goldhill, *Reading Greek Tragedy*, p. 145; Hesk, *Deception and Democracy*, pp. 24-9.

7. See Pavlovskis, 'Voice of the Actor', pp. 116-17. However, we cannot be sure that the distribution of parts 'was ever arranged for this kind of dramatic purpose' in Greek tragic performances (Garvie, *Ajax*, p. 216). Another problem here is that the 'three-actor rule' was such an embedded convention that audiences may not have marked the fact that the same actor played Ajax and Teucer (or, say, Athena and Menelaus) as in any way significant.

8. See also *Iliad* 18.132-7 where Ajax is compared to a lion protecting his young as he defends Patroclus' body with his broad shield.

9. See Euripides *Helen* 90-104 and Horace *Odes* 1.7.21-32

10. This argument cannot be proved conclusively, but it is attractive to see Sophocles forging a link between Attic Salamis and Cypriot Salamis through the figure of Teucer – a tragic exile of mixed identity. Herodotus stresses the manner in which the Cypriot communities blend Greek and non-Greek identities and customs (7.90).

11. Blundell, *Helping Friends*, p. 81.

12. Blundell, *Helping Friends*, p. 80.

13. In Homer's version (*Iliad* 22.395-404, 464; 24.15) Hector is already dead *before* Achilles ties him to the chariot rail and there is no mention of him doing so with the belt. March, 'Sophocles' *Ajax*', p. 17, suggests that Sophocles has invented this more gruesome death for Hector but it may have been an alternative version in the Epic Cycle.

14. Here I am countering a view that Teucer's reflections on fate and the divine are 'trite' (Stanford, *Ajax*, p. 191). It should also be noted that some scholars bracket lines 1028-39 of Teucer's speech as a later, perhaps fourth-century, addition. See Lloyd-Jones and Wilson, *Sophoclea*, pp. 32-3. It is always possible that the lines were added for a revival of the play, but the usual grounds for saying this are that they contain too much bombast or deep reflection in comparison with the rest of the speech. I just do not see this myself.

15. Tecmessa and Ajax have technically engaged in the first *agôn* at 430-544. Their debating is indirect and disjointed in comparison with 1047-162. See Holt, 'Debate Scenes', p. 277.

16. A massive bibliography could be given. On the formal *agôn* in tragedy, see Duchemin, *L'Agon*, and Lloyd, *Agôn in Euripides*. On the debate-scenes of our play see especially Holt, 'Debate Scenes', and Barker, 'Fall-out from Dissent'. On the interaction between tragedy and Athenian rhetorical practice (and theory) see Buxton, *Persuasion*; Goldhill, *Reading Greek Tragedy*, pp. 222-42; Ober and Strauss, 'Drama, Political Rhetoric'; Hall, 'Lawcourt Dramas'.

17. It is true, however, that once Ajax is deluded he seems to think that he is slaughtering members of the army in general (53, 95). See Garvie, *Ajax*, p. 197

18. Denying burial was regarded as transgressive on the grounds that it would invite pollution. Relatives would be allowed to bury even a traitor's body beyond the aggrieved city-state's frontier. For the nuances, see Parker, *Miasma*, pp. 44-7; Fisher, *Hybris*, pp. 311, 318-19. On the *hubris* of the Atreids see p. 122.

19. As Dutta, *Ajax*, p. 76 points out, there is little hint of an unruly or unheeding Ajax in the *Iliad*.

20. Heath, *Poetics of Greek Tragedy*, p. 200.

21. For the Athenian construction of the Spartans as duplicitous, over-reliant on military training, lacking in courage, giving their women too much freedom and much more besides see Hesk, *Deception and Democracy*, pp. 23-40.

22. See Griffin, 'Sophocles and the Democratic City'.

23. Rose, 'Historicizing Sophocles' *Ajax*'.

24. Stanford, *Ajax*, p. 198. As Stanford points out, the Athenians had been resenting Spartan interference in their affairs ever since the expulsion of Hippias the Peisistratid. Teucer's attack on Menelaus has parallels in Euripides: see *Andromache* 581-2 and *Telephus* fragment 723 ('You have got Sparta, govern it'). This does not make the *Telephus* line a model for 1102 and hence does not mean that *Ajax* was performed after 438 BC. But as Garvie, *Ajax*, p. 225 points out, the attack on Spartan acquisitiveness became proverbial.

25. See Coray, *Wissen und Erkennen*, pp. 394-9.

26. See also Cleon's emphasis on the rule of law and the importance of *sôphrosunê* at Thucydides 3.37.3.

27. For the text of the oath, see Siewert, 'Ephebic Oath', pp. 102-3.

28. See Vidal-Naquet, *Fragments*, p. 79.

29. Here, I am drawing on Blundell, *Helping Friends*, pp. 122-7, and Foley, 'Tragedy and Democratic Ideology', p. 137.

30. As Tom Harrison points out to me, Menelaus' wish to deny

Ajax's body respectful treatment contrasts with the views of the Spartan General Pausanias at Herodotus 9.79-80. Pausanias rebukes Lampon for suggesting that the Greeks abuse Persian bodies as revenge for the way that Leonidas was treated. Pausanias sees mistreatment of bodies as a barbarian trait.

31. Teucer repeats Menelaus' 'killing me' (*kteinanta*:1125) at 1126: 'killing you?' (*kteinanta*). He echoes Menelaus' 'god is my saviour' (*theos eksôizei*: 1128) at 1129: 'Do not dishonour the gods if it is by the gods that you were saved' (*theous, theois sesômenos*). He repeats Menelaus' word for enemy (*polemios*): 1132-3. He trumps Menelaus' 'this man must not be buried' (*ouchi thapteon*) with 'he *shall* be buried (*tethapsetai*) (1140-1). Finally, *aischiston* ('most shameful': 1161) contemptuously repeats *aischron* (1159).

32. *Dikaia* at 1126 picks up *dikaiôi* at 1125. And at 1134 Menelaus counters Teucer's quibble that Ajax can't have been Menelaus' *polemios* by switching into different terms for hatred and providing the jingle *misount'emisei*.

33. In both Homeric epic and fifth-century culture, archery is generally deemed to be less honourable than face-to-face fighting with a sword or spear. But arguments about the relative merits of 'hoplitism' and archery in tragedy and philosophy suggest that there was some fifth-century concern to re-examine the automatic assumption that 'Ajaxian/Achillean' fighting and its classical, collective, hoplite counterpart were the best and most manly modes of engagement. See Euripides *Hercules Furens* 161ff. and Plato *Laches* 190e5-191e1. Teucer's proud statement that archery is not 'vulgar' (*banauson*) is interesting because *banausos* is a prosaic word which occurs only here in extant tragedy. Teucer is perhaps referring to the fact that his bow and arrows were gifts from Apollo (*Iliad* 15.440-1). But does his 'untragic' diction make him sound 'banausic'?

34. Menelaus' nautical fable inverts that of Eteocles at Aeschylus *Seven Against Thebes* 602-4. Critics argue that the fable is a rhetorical device of 'low character' (Fraenkel, *Agamemnon*, pp. 773-4; Heath, *Poetics of Greek Tragedy*, p. 200). It was certainly a 'popular' genre of speech and is probably to be associated with verbal duelling.

35. For 'laconic' Laconians (Spartans), see Herodotus 3.46.1-2. See also Plutarch's *Spartan Sayings* in Talbert, *Plutarch on Sparta*, along with Harrison, 'Herodotus' Conception of Foreign Languages'.

36. Here, I echo the view of Heath, *Poetics of Greek Tragedy*, p. 206.

37. See Parks, *Verbal Duelling*, and Martin, *Language of Heroes*.

38. Thus Stanford, *Ajax*, p. 203, was wrong to complain that Teucer's mocking repetitions mark him as inferior to Ajax and contribute to the 'unheroic' and 'low' tone of the debate scenes.

39. See Herzfeld, *Poetics of Manhood*, pp. 136-49.

40. See Hesk, 'Verbal Duelling', on the ways in which this exchange and Athenian dramatic 'flyting' in general might engage with Athenian culture's ambivalent legal and political confrontation with verbal duelling, abuse and games involving improvised flyting and capping. For all its crowd-pleasing panache, Teucer's duelling may contain the sort of abusive speech which Athenian legal discourse associated with extra-judicial feuding and violence.

41. See Burian, 'Supplication and Hero Cult'; Henrichs, 'The Tomb of Aias'.

42. Garvie, *Ajax*, p. 231.

43. The Chorus are not thinking of a specific person here. The idea that there is a 'first inventor' for various (often unpleasant) aspects of human life is a commonplace in Greek and Roman poetry. See Kleingünther, *'Prôtos Heuretês'*.

44. See Euripides *Hippolytus* 732-51, *Helen* 1479-86, *Bacchae* 402-16.

45. Segal, *Tragedy and Civilization*, p. 146.

46. Stanford, *Ajax*, p. 205.

47. For sophistic rhetoric's fondness for flexing its muscles on mythology see Gorgias' *Encomium of Helen* and *Defence of Palamedes*; Aristophanes *Clouds* 1078-81.

48. The *Ajax*'s interest in the meaning and value of *sôphrosunê* is paralleled in other Greek tragedies. See Euripides' *Hippolytus* and Mills, *Hippolytus*, pp. 70-3.

49. As Garvie, *Ajax*, p. 131, points out, the word *anêr* is used 80 times in this play – the nearest contender is *Oedipus Tyrannus* with 60 occurrences.

50. The *polyptoton* '*monos monou*' recasts the emphatic repetition and juxtaposition of 'alone' which Ajax used at 467.

51. Blundell, *Helping Friends*, p. 100, departs from Segal, *Tragedy and Civilization*, p. 133, in seeing the contrast between Ajax and Odysseus as a 'chronological one' because the contrast begins with Homer. But it is clear to me that Agamemnon is encouraging an audience to see Ajax as polis-hostile, so this chronological rhetoric is informing the play.

52. Blundell, *Helping Friends*, p. 105.

53. The importance of the word/deed distinction is pointed out by Blundell, *Helping Friends*, p. 95.

54. In this and the next paragraph my analysis in indebted to that of Blundell, *Helping Friends*, pp. 96-105.

55. Blundell, *Helping Friends*, p. 96.

56. Barker, 'Fall-out from Dissent', rather cleverly puts the Chorus and the the audience at the centre of the final scenes' meaning. He points out that the Chorus 'fail to endorse fully the position of any of the duelling characters' and sees this intense focus on spectating and assessing the double *agôn* as a reflection of the new social conditions of democracy: 'in short, the play explores how the hero's dissent is democratized'. Like Worman, 'Odysseus *Panourgos*', Barker is more suspicious of Odysseus' strategy of negotiation than I am. Both are certainly right to characterise Odysseus' ruse as one of mirroring the prejudices of Agamemnon.

57. See Blundell, *Helping Friends*, pp. 100-5.

7. Criticism and Reception

1. See Knox, *Heroic Temper*; Winnington-Ingram, *Sophocles: an Interpretation*; Goldhill, *Reading Greek Tragedy*, pp. 154-67; Segal, *Sophocles' Tragic World*, pp. 1-15.

2. See Halliwell, *Aristotle's Poetics*, p. 217.

3. See Halliwell, *Aristotle's Poetics*, pp. 223-4.

4. On this, see Jones, *Aristotle and Greek Tragedy*, pp. 11-20; Goldhill, *Reading Greek Tragedy*, p. 171.

5. Goldhill, *Reading Greek Tragedy*, p. 172.

6. Halliwell, *Aristotle's Poetics*, p. 139.

7. Jones, *Aristotle and Greek Tragedy*, p. 45

8. Taplin, *Stagecraft of* Aeschylus, p. 312. Goldhill, *Reading Greek Tragedy*, pp. 170-1, sees affinities between Jones's and Taplin's views and those of Tycho von Wilamowitz who believed that Sophocles had no interest in character consistency.

9. This is pointed out in Easterling, 'Character in Sophocles', and in Easterling, 'Constructing Character'.

10. See Gould, 'Dramatic Character'.

11. Goldhill, *Reading Greek Tragedy*, pp. 180-98.

12. For more on these debates, see Pelling, *Characterization and Individuality*, and Gill, *Personality*.

13. Goldhill, *Reading Greek Tragedy*, p. 155.

14. These quotations are from Knox, *Heroic Temper*, pp. 18, 21 and 27.

15. See above, pp. 62-3, 84-6 and Gill, *Personality*, pp. 206-13.

16. On the 'pietist' approach, see above, pp. 59-60.

17. My use of 'slightly' is studied – Knox and Gill are too good as scholars for their readings of *Ajax* to be limited by *complete* adherence to Romantic or Aristotelian notions of heroism and character. But there are *tendencies* in their readings which are illustrative and useful for my own purposes.

18. In many (but not all) places, this section is indebted to the excellent discussion of Goldhill, *Reading Greek Tragedy*, pp. 168-98.

19. Garvie, *Ajax*, p. 156.

20. See Stanford, *Ajax*, pp. 104-5; Kamerbeek, *Ajax*, p. 81.

21. Jebb, *Ajax*, p. 60.

22. Some manuscripts attribute this line to the Chorus or Chorus-leader.

23. Goldhill, *Reading Greek Tragedy*, p. 185.

24. For further debate and discussion of Ajax's state of mind and the imagery used of his madness see Biggs, 'Disease Theme'; Holt, 'Ajax' Ailment'; Goldhill, *Reading Greek Tragedy*, pp. 168-98; Garvie, *Ajax*.

25. Knox, *Word and Action*, pp. 150-1.

26. Zanker, '*Ajax* and Heroic Values', p. 21.

27. Winnington-Ingram, *Sophocles: an Interpretation*, p. 19.

28. Goldhill, *Reading Greek Tragedy*, p. 156.

29. Goldhill, *Reading Greek Tragedy*, p. 156.

30. See Bowra, *Sophoclean Tragedy*, pp. 27-38; Kitto, *Form and Meaning*, pp. 179-98; Kirkwood, *A Study*, p. 274; Webster, *Introduction to Sophocles*, p. 65.

31. Garvie, *Ajax*, p. 13.

32. Fisher, *Hybris*, p. 1.

33. See Fisher, *Hybris*, p. 497.

34. See Wilson, 'Demosthenes 21'.

35. On the law against *hubris* (*graphê hubreôs*), see MacDowell, '*Hybris* in Athens'; Fisher, *Hybris*, pp. 36-85.

36. See Cairns, '*Hybris*, Dishonour and Thinking Big'.

37. This list is indebted to that in Fisher, *Hybris*, p. 312.

38. Garvie, *Ajax*, p. 136.

39. Garvie, *Ajax*, pp. 136-7.

40. Segal, *Tragedy and Civilization*, p. 119.

41. It has been argued that 1061 is an interpolation and hence not part of the original text. See Reeve, 'Interpolation', p. 161 and Fisher, *Hybris*, pp. 314-15.

42. See Fisher, *Hybris*, pp. 86-151.

43. Garvie, *Ajax*, pp. 196-7.

44. See Fisher, *Hybris*, p. 506.

45. Fisher, *Hybris*, p. 509.

46. See Hesiod fragment 30; Sophocles *Seven Against Thebes* 387ff.; Euripides *Phoenician Women* 180ff.

47. Jebb, *Ajax*, p. xlvii.

48. The most accessible translation of Antisthenes' *Ajax* and *Odysseus* can be found in Gagarin and Woodruff, *Early Greek Political Thought*, pp. 167-72. Greek text and commentary is in Decleva Caizzi, *Antisthenis Fragmenta*. For relevant discussion, see Rankin, *Antisthenes Sokratikos*; Hesk, *Deception and Democracy*, pp. 118-21; Worman, 'Odysseus *Panourgos*'.

49. Seneca tells us that Ovid was so keen a student of Latro (a famous declamation expert) that he used this teacher's maxims in his own poetry. As an example he cites *Metamorphoses* 13.121-2 and says it originated with Latro (Seneca *Controversiae* 2.2.8).

50. Hardie, 'Ovid and Early Imperial Literature', p. 37.

51. Hardie, 'Ovid and Early Imperial Literature', p. 37.

52. On Ajax's anger, see Hopkinson, *Ovid Metamorphoses Book XIII*, pp. 18-20.

53. For this, see the excellent Lyne, *Ovid's Changing Worlds*.

54. Dearing (ed.), *Works of John Dryden*, vol. VII, p. 449.

55. See *LIMC* 1.1.314-36 for a full inventory and discussion of ancient visual art representing Ajax.

56. Hartt, *Giulio Romano*, p. 181.

57. For details and plates of most of the pictures, see Schiff, *Johann Heinrich Fuseli 1741-1825*, nos 325, 390, 391, 1196, and 1253.

58. Craske, *Art in Europe 1700-1830*, p. 42.

59. Becker, *The Mad Genius Controversy*, p. 149.

60. Craske, *Art in Europe 1700-1830*, p. 242.

61. See Macintosh 'Tragedy in Performance', and Burian, 'Tragedy Adapted'.

62. See Macintosh, 'Tragedy in Performance', p. 292. In the 1882 production, J.K. Stephen played Ajax. Stephen was a cousin of Virginia Woolf and became a fellow of King's College Cambridge. He was a friend of the Greek scholar Walter Headlam and in 1891 wrote a defence of the compulsory study of Greek at Cambridge. A year later he went mad and starved himself to death. As Goldhill, *Who Needs Greek?*, p. 241, remarks, 'briefly he was the chief suspect for being Jack the Ripper, which makes his performance as the mad murderer Ajax, in the first Cambridge Greek Play, seem particularly apt'. A photograph of Stephen in his Ajax costume, looking wistful rather than mad, is reproduced in Dutta, *Ajax*, p. 54.

63. On modernity and 'madness' see Foucault, *Madness and Civilization*.

64. I have learned about this from Hartigan, *Greek Tragedy on the American Stage*, pp. 118-20.

65. These quotes are from the *New York Daily Mirror*, 2 April 1904, as cited by Hartigan, *Greek Tragedy on the American Stage*, p. 119.

66. Sellars, 'Talk at Carnuntum', pp. 94-5.

67. McDonald, *Ancient Sun*, p. 77.

68. This quote from Auletta's unpublished script is from McDonald, *Ancient Sun*, p. 77.

69. Sellars, 'Talk at Carnuntum', p. 99.

70. Wilders (ed.), *Samuel Butler: Hudibras*, p. xxvii.

71. Sellars, 'Talk at Carnuntum', p. 99.

72. McDonald, *Ancient Sun*, p. 82.

73. See Hardwick, *Translating Worlds, Translating Cultures*, pp. 63-78.

Guide to Further Reading

Translations

In this book I have drawn on the prose translation of Garvie, *Ajax*, and the verse translation of Dutta, *Ajax* (see bibliography for full details). Both are accurate, readable and keyed to the Greek text's original line-numbers. Another excellent verse translation is that of Golder and Pevear, *Ajax* (see bibliography). All these translations have substantial notes suitable for the reader in translation. The facing translation of Jebb, *Ajax*, is also very usable.

Editions/commentaries

Garvie, *Ajax*, offers an introduction, text, translation and commentary which is excellent. But see Rosenbloom, 'Ajax is *Megas*', for a good review article which points to Garvie's 'hero-worshipping' tendencies. Stanford, *Ajax*, is still widely available and while the commentary would be difficult for the Greekless reader, the introduction and appendices are good for all. Jebb, *Ajax*, is currently being revamped by Peter Wilson and stands the test of time remarkably well. Kamerbeek, *Ajax*, is a commentary without text and its heavily philological emphasis makes it unfriendly to undergraduates.

Book-length studies containing material on *Ajax*

Buxton, *Sophocles*, is brief but gives an excellent overview of Sophoclean tragedy and some fine pointers for our play. The following are essential for getting to grips with key areas of controversy: Knox, *Word and Action* (good on Ajax's extremism); Taplin, *Greek Tragedy in Action* (good on staging difficulties and significant objects such as the sword); Winnington-Ingram, *Sophocles: an Interpretation* (refines Knox's formulation persuasively); Heath, *Poetics of Greek Tragedy* (particularly good on the post-suicide scenes); Goldhill, *Reading Greek Tragedy* (detailed exploration of Ajax's madness and 'character' issues); Blundell, *Helping Friends* (on theme of *philia*); Gill, *Personality* (interesting on Ajax's motivation and sense of justice).

184

Guide to Further Reading

The *Ajax* and Homer

The following books and articles deal with our play's 'recasting' of Homeric epic and Homeric values: Knox, *Heroic Temper*, and *Word and Action*; Kirkwood, *A Study*; Winnington-Ingram, *Sophocles: an Interpretation*; Easterling, 'Tragic Homer' (very good on intertextuality with *Iliad* 6); Goldhill, *Reading Greek Tragedy* and 'Great Dionysia'; Zanker, '*Ajax* and Heroic Values' (argues against prevalent view that *Ajax* instantiates values which are different from those found in Homer); Gill, *Personality* (also sees affinities between Homeric heroic gestures and those of Sophocles' Ajax).

The *Ajax* and hero-cult

On hero-cult in Attica generally, see Kearns, *Heroes of Attica*. On hero-cult in our play see Burian, 'Supplication and Hero Cult' (a detailed case for seeing the play as aetiology for Ajax's cult); Henrichs, 'Tomb of Aias'; Seaford, *Reciprocity and Ritual* (relates the play to an entire theory of tragedy's close relationship with civic ritual).

The *Ajax* and Athenian democracy

Rose, 'Historicizing Sophocles' *Ajax*', plausibly relates the play to Athenian imperialism and elite generalship. Readings of the play in terms of Athenian democratic ideology: Sorum, '*Ajax* in context'; Goldhill, 'Great Dionysia'; Meier, *Political Art of Greek Tragedy*; Barker, 'Fall-out from Dissent'.

Other recommended studies

For useful perspectives on the nature and imagery of Ajax's suicide, see Cohen, 'Imagery'; Belfiore, *Murder Among Friends*, and Loraux, *Tragic Ways*. Belfiore's book and Blundell, *Helping Friends*, discuss the play's themes of friendship, loyalty and enmity. On the themes of *hubris*, honour and shame, see Fisher, *Hybris*, and Cairns, *Aidôs*. Moore, 'Dissembling Speech', and Sicherl, 'Tragic Issue', give a good sense of the issues surrounding the deception speech.

Reception of the *Ajax*

Hopkinson, *Ovid Metamorphosis Book XIII*, is helpful on Roman and Ovidian reception. For Fuseli and neo-Classicism in art, see Craske, *Art in Europe 1700-1830*. Macintosh, 'Tragedy in Performance', gives an overview of the performance of tragedy in the nineteenth

185

and twentieth centuries. McDonald, *Ancient Sun*, and Hartigan, *Greek Tragedy on the American Stage*, discuss the two American productions.

Bibliography

D = M. Davies (editor), *Epicorum Graecorum Fragmenta* (Göttingen: Vandenhoeck & Ruprecht, 1988).

D-K = H. Diels and W. Kranz (editors), *Die Fragmente der Vorsokratiker*, 6th ed. (Dublin: Weidmann, 1951).

FGrH = F. Jacoby (editor) *Fragmente der grieschischen Historiker* (Berlin: Weidmann and Leiden: E.J. Brill, 1923-1958).

K-A = R. Kassel and C. Austin (editors) *Poetae Comici Graeci* (Berlin: de Gruyter, 1984-).

L = H.G. Evelyn-White, *Hesiod, The Homeric Hymns and Homerica*, Loeb Classical Library (Cambridge MA: Harvard University Press, 1914).

LIMC = *Lexicon Iconographicum Mythologiae Classicae* (Zürich: Artemis, 1981-).

TGrF = B. Snell, R. Kannicht, S. Radt (editors) *Tragicorum Graecorum Fragmenta*, 4 vols (Göttingen: Vandenhoeck & Ruprecht, 1971-1986).

L. Abel, *Metatheatre: a New View of Dramatic Form* (New York: Hill and Wang, 1963).

A. Adkins, *Merit and Responsibility: a Study of Greek Values* (Oxford: Clarendon Press, 1960).

W. Allan, *The Andromache and Euripidean Tragedy* (Oxford: Oxford University Press, 2000).

E. Barker, 'The Fall-out from Dissent: Hero and Audience in Sophocles' *Ajax*', *Greece and Rome* (forthcoming).

G. Becker, *The Mad Genius Controversy: a Study in the Sociology of Deviance* (London, Sage: 1978).

E. Belfiore, *Murder Among Friends. Violation of Philia in Greek Tragedy* (Oxford: Oxford University Press, 2000).

P. Biggs, 'The Disease Theme in Sophocles' *Ajax, Philoctetes*, and *Trachiniae*', *Classical Philology* (1961), pp. 223-35.

M. Blundell, *Helping Friends and Harming Enemies: a Study in Sophocles and Greek Ethics* (Cambridge: Cambridge University Press, 1989).

A. Bowie, 'The End of Sophocles' *Ajax*', *Liverpool Classical Monthly* (1983), pp. 114-15.

C. Bowra, *Sophoclean Tragedy* (Oxford: Clarendon Press, 1944).

Bibliography

———— *Greek Lyric Poetry* (Oxford: Clarendon Press, 1961).

D. Bradshaw, 'The Ajax Myth and the Polis: Old Values and New', in D. Pozzi and J. Wickersham (editors), *Myth and the Polis* (Ithaca, NY: Cornell University Press, 1991), pp. 99-125.

N. Brown, 'Pindar, Sophocles, and the Thirty Years' Peace', *Transactions of the American Philological Association* 82 (1951), pp. 1-28.

K. Brušák, 'Signs in the Chinese Theatre', in L. Matejka and I. Titunik (editors), *Semiotics of Art: Prague School Contributions* (Cambridge, MA: Harvard University Press), pp. 59-73.

P. Burian, 'Supplication and Hero Cult in Sophocles' *Ajax*', *Greek, Roman and Byzantine Studies* 13 (1972), pp. 151-6.

———— 'Myth into *Muthos*: the Shaping of Tragic Plot', in Easterling, *Cambridge Companion*, pp. 178-210.

———— 'Tragedy Adapted for Stages and Screens: the Renaissance to the Present', in Easterling, *Cambridge Companion*, pp. 228-83.

A. Burnett, *Revenge in Attic and Later Tragedy* (Berkeley, University of California Press, 1998).

R. Buxton, *Persuasion in Greek Tragedy: a Study of 'Peitho'* (Cambridge: Cambridge University Press, 1982).

———— *Imaginary Greece: the Contexts of Mythology* (Cambridge: Cambridge University Press, 1994).

———— *Sophocles: Greece and Rome New Surveys in the Classics* (Oxford: Oxford University Press, 1995).

D. Cairns, *Aidôs: the Psychology and Ethics of Honour and Shame in Ancient Greek Literature* (Oxford: Clarendon Press, 1993).

———— 'Hybris, Dishonour and Thinking Big', *Journal of Hellenic Studies*, 116 (1996), pp. 1-32.

D. Campbell, *Greek Lyric*, vol. 5: *The New School of Poetry and Anonymous Songs and Hymns*, Loeb Classical Library (Cambridge MA: Harvard University Press, 1993).

C. Carpenter and T. Faraone (editors), *Masks of Dionysus* (Ithaca, NY: Cornell University Press, 1993).

P. Cartledge, *The Greeks* (Oxford: Oxford University Press, 1993).

———— ' "Deep Plays": Theatre as Process in Greek Civic Life', in Easterling, *Cambridge Companion*, pp. 3-35.

D. Cohen, 'The Imagery of Sophocles: a Study of Ajax's Suicide', *Greece and Rome* 25 (1978), pp. 24-36.

M. Coray, *Wissen und Erkennen bei Sophokles* (Basle: Reinhardt, 1993).

M. Craske, *Art in Europe 1700-1830* (Oxford: Oxford University Press, 1997).

E. Csapo and W. Slater, *The Context of Ancient Drama* (Ann Arbor: University of Michigan Press, 1994).

G. Dalmeyda, 'Sophocle, Ajax', *Revue des Études Grecques* 46 (1933), pp. 1-14.

Bibliography

J. Daly, *Horizontal Resonance as a Principle of Composition in the Plays of Sophocles* (New York: Garland, 1990).

J. Davidson, 'The Parodos of Sophocles' *Ajax*', *Bulletin of the Institute of Classical Studies* 22 (1975), pp. 163-77.

M. Davies, *The Epic Cycle* (Bristol: Bristol Classical Press, 1989).

M. Davis, 'Politics and Madness', in P. Euben (editor), *Greek Tragedy and Political Theory* (Berkeley: University of California Press, 1986), pp. 142-61.

V. Dearing (editor), *The Works of John Dryden*, vol. VII: *Poems 1697-1700* (Berkeley: University of California Press, 2000).

F. Decleva Caizzi, *Antisthenis Fragmenta* (Milan: Istituto editorale Cisalpino, 1966).

H. Diller, *Gottheit und Mensch in der Tragödie des Sophokles* (Darmstadt: Wissenschaftliche Buchgesellschaft, 1963).

G. Dobrov, *Figures of Play: Greek Drama and Metafictional Poetics* (Oxford: Oxford University Press, 2001).

K. Dover, *Greek Popular Morality in the Time of Plato and Aristotle* (Oxford: Oxford University Press, 1974).

K. Dowden 'Homer's Sense of Text', *Journal of Hellenic Studies* 116 (1996), pp. 47-61.

J. Duchemin, *L'Agon dans la Tragédie Grecque* (Paris: Les Belles Lettres, 1968).

S. Dutta, *Sophocles: Ajax*, Cambridge Translations from Greek Drama (Cambridge: Cambridge University Press, 2001).

P.E. Easterling, 'Character in Sophocles', *Greece and Rome* 24 (1977), pp. 121-9.

────── 'The Tragic Homer', *Bulletin of the Institute of Classical Studies* 31 (1984), pp. 1-8.

────── 'Constructing Character in Greek Tragedy', in Pelling, *Characterization and Individuality*, pp. 83-99.

────── 'A Show for Dionysus', in Easterling, *Cambridge Companion*, pp. 36-53.

────── (editor), *Cambridge Companion to Greek Tragedy* (Cambridge: Cambridge University Press, 1997).

P.E. Easterling and E. Hall (editors), *Greek and Roman Actors* (Cambridge: Cambridge University Press, 2002).

J. Evans, 'A Reading of Sophocles' *Ajax*', *Quaderni Urbinati di Cultura Classica* 38 (1991), pp. 69-85.

T. Falkner, 'Making a Spectacle of Oneself: the Metatheatrical Design of Sophocles' *Ajax*', *Text and Presentation: The Journal of the Comparative Drama Conference* 14 (1993), pp. 35-40.

────── 'Scholars Versus Actors: Text and Performance in the Greek Tragic Scholia', in Easterling and Hall, *Greek and Roman Actors*, pp. 342-61.

J. Ferguson, 'Ambiguity in *Ajax*', *Dioniso* 44 (1970), pp. 12-29.

Bibliography

N. Fisher, *Hybris: a Study in the Values of Honour and Shame in Ancient Greece* (Warminster: Aris and Phillips, 1992).

H. Foley, 'Tragedy and Democratic Ideology: the Case of Sophocles' *Antigone*', in Goff, *History, Tragedy, Theory*, pp. 131-50.

—— *Female Acts in Greek Tragedy* (Princeton: Princeton University Press, 2001).

M. Foucault, *Madness and Civilization* (New York: Random House, 1965).

E. Fraenkel, *Agamemnon*, 3 vols (Oxford: Oxford University Press, 1950).

R. Friedrich, 'Everything to do with Dionysus?' in Silk, *Tragedy and the Tragic*, pp. 257-83.

M. Gagarin and P. Woodruff, *Early Greek Political Thought from Homer to the Sophists* (Cambridge: Cambridge University Press, 1995).

C. Gardiner, *The Sophoclean Chorus* (Iowa City: University Press of Iowa, 1987).

A. Garvie, *Sophocles: Ajax* (Warminster: Aris and Phillips, 1998).

H. Gasti, 'Sophocles *Ajax*: the military *hubris*', *Quaderni Urbinati di Cultura Classica* 40 (1992), pp. 81-93.

G. Gellie, *Sophocles: a Reading* (Carlton: Melbourne University Press, 1972).

C. Gill, *Personality in Greek Epic, Tragedy and Philosophy* (Oxford: Clarendon Press, 1996).

B. Goff (editor), *History, Tragedy, Theory: Dialogues in Athenian Drama* (Austin: University of Texas Press, 1995).

H. Golder and R. Pevear, *Sophocles: Aias (Ajax)* (New York and Oxford: Oxford University Press, 1999).

S. Goldhill, *Reading Greek Tragedy* (Cambridge: Cambridge University Press, 1988).

—— 'The Great Dionysia and Civic Ideology', in Winkler and Zeitlin, *Nothing to do with Dionysus?*, pp. 97-129.

—— *The Poet's Voice* (Cambridge: Cambridge University Press, 1991).

—— 'Representing Democracy: Women at the Great Dionysia', in Osborne and Hornblower, *Ritual, Finance, Politics*, pp. 347-69.

—— 'Collectivity and Otherness. The Authority of the Tragic Chorus. Response to Gould', in Silk, *Tragedy and the Tragic*, pp. 244-56.

—— 'Modern Critical Approaches to Greek Tragedy' in Easterling, *Cambridge Companion*, pp. 324-47.

—— 'Civic Ideology and the Problem of Difference: the Politics of Aeschylean Tragedy, Once Again', *Journal of Hellenic Studies* 120 (2000), pp. 34-56.

—— *Who Needs Greek?* (Cambridge: Cambridge University Press, 2002).

J. Gould, 'Dramatic Character and "Human Intelligibility" in Greek Tragedy', *Proceedings of the Cambridge Philological Society* 24 (1978), pp. 43-67.

―――― 'Sophocles', in S. Hornblower and A. Spawforth (editors) *Oxford Classical Dictionary* (Oxford: Oxford University Press 1996), pp. 1422-5.

―――― 'Tragedy and Collective Experience', in Silk, *Tragedy and the Tragic*, pp. 217-43.

―――― 'Myth, Memory and the Chorus: "Tragic Rationality" ', in R. Buxton (editor), *From Myth to Reason?* (Oxford: Oxford University Press, 1999), pp. 107-18.

H. Grégoire and P. Orgels, 'L'*Ajax* de Sophocle, Alcibiade et Sparte', *Annuaire de l'Institut de philologie et d'histoire orientale et slave* 13 (1953), pp. 653-63.

J. Griffin, 'The Social Function of Attic Tragedy', *Classical Quarterly* 48 (1998), pp. 39-61.

―――― 'Sophocles and the Democratic City', in J. Griffin (editor), *Sophocles Revisited* (Oxford: Oxford University Press, 1999), pp. 73-94.

M. Griffith, 'Brilliant Dynasts: Power and Politics in the *Oresteia*', *Classical Antiquity* 14 (1995), pp. 62-129.

―――― 'The King and Eye: the Rule of the Father in Greek Tragedy', *Proceedings of the Cambridge Philological Society* 44 (1998), pp. 20-84.

E. Hall, *Inventing the Barbarian: Greek Self-Definition through Tragedy* (Oxford: Oxford University Press, 1989).

―――― 'Lawcourt Dramas: the Power of Performance in Greek Forensic Oratory', *Bulletin of the Institute of Classical Studies* 40 (1995), pp. 39-58.

―――― *Aeschylus: Persians* (Warminster: Aris and Phillips, 1996).

―――― 'The Singing Actors of Antiquity', in Easterling and Hall, *Greek and Roman Actors*, pp. 3-38.

S. Halliwell, *Aristotle's Poetics*, 2nd ed. (London: Duckworth, 1998).

P. Hardie, 'Ovid and Early Imperial Literature', in P. Hardie (editor), *Cambridge Companion to Ovid* (Cambridge: Cambridge University Press, 2002), pp. 34-45.

L. Hardwick, *Translating Worlds, Translating Cultures* (London: Duckworth, 2000).

T. Harrison, 'Herodotus' Conception of Foreign Languages', *Histos* 2 (1998), www.dur.ac.uk/Classics/Histos.

―――― *The Emptiness of Asia: Aeschylus' Persians and the History of the Fifth Century* (London: Duckworth, 2000).

―――― (editor), *Greeks and Barbarians* (Edinburgh: Edinburgh University Press, 2002).

K. Hartigan, *Greek Tragedy on the American Stage: Ancient Drama in the Commercial Theater, 1882-1994* (Westport: Greenwood Press, 1995).

F. Hartt, *Giulio Romano* (New Haven: Yale University Press, 1958).

M. Heath, *The Poetics of Greek Tragedy* (London: Duckworth, 1987).

A. Henrichs, 'The Tomb of Aias and the Prospect of Hero Cult in Sophokles', *Classical Antiquity* 12 (1993), pp. 165-80.

M. Herzfeld, *The Poetics of Manhood: Contest and Identity in a Cretan Mountain Village* (Princeton: Princeton University Press, 1985).

J. Hesk, *Deception and Democracy in Classical Athens* (Cambridge: Cambridge University Press, 2000).

——— 'Verbal Duelling and Civic Discourse in Athenian Culture', (forthcoming).

S. Hinds, *Allusion and Intertext* (Cambridge: Cambridge University Press, 1998).

P. Holt, 'Ajax's Ailment', *Ramus* 9 (1980), pp. 22-33.

——— 'The Debate Scenes in the *Ajax*', *American Journal of Philology* 113 (1992), 319-31.

N. Hopkinson, *Ovid Metamorphoses Book XIII* (Cambridge: Cambridge University Press, 2000).

J. Hubert, *Metatheater: the Example of Shakespeare* (Lincoln: University of Nebraska Press, 1991).

R. Jebb, *Sophocles: the Plays and Fragments, Part VII: Ajax* (Cambridge: Cambridge University Press, 1896).

J. Jones, *On Aristotle and Greek Tragedy* (London: Chatto and Windus, 1962).

J. Kamerbeek, *Sophocles, the Plays*, vol. 1: *Ajax*, 2nd ed. (Leiden: E.J. Brill, 1963).

E. Kearns, *The Heroes of Attica*, Supplement 47 of the *Bulletin of the Institute of Classical Studies* (London: Institute of Classical Studies, 1989).

G. Kirkwood, *A Study in Sophoclean Drama* (Ithaca, NY: Cornell University Press, 1958).

——— 'Homer and Sophocles' Ajax', in M. Anderson (editor), *Classical Drama and its Influence* (London: Methuen, 1965).

H. Kitto, *Form and Meaning in Drama* (London: Macmillan, 1956).

A. Kleingünther, *'Prôtos Heuretês'*, *Philologus Supplement* 26 (Leipzig, 1933).

B. Knox, *The Heroic Temper: Studies in Sophoclean Tragedy* (Berkeley: University of California Press, 1964).

——— *Word and Action: Essays in the Ancient Theatre* (Baltimore, Johns Hopkins University Press, 1979).

D. Konstan, 'Greek Friendship', *American Journal of* Philology 117 (1996), pp. 71-94.

——— *Friendship in the Classical World* (Cambridge: Cambridge University Press, 1997).

Bibliography

M. Lefkowitz, *The Lives of the Greek Poets* (London: Duckworth, 1981).

M. Lloyd, *The Agôn in Euripides* (Oxford: Clarendon Press, 1992).

H. Lloyd-Jones and N. Wilson, *Sophoclea: Studies on the Text of Sophocles* (Oxford: Clarendon Press, 1990).

N. Loraux, *The Invention of Athens* (Princeton: Princeton University Press, 1986).

—— *Tragic Ways of Killing a Woman* (Cambridge MA: Harvard University Press, 1987).

R. Lyne, *Ovid's Changing Worlds: English Metamorphoses 1572-1632* (Oxford: Oxford University Press, 2001).

L. McClure, *Spoken Like a Woman: Speech and Gender in Athenian Drama* (Princeton: Princeton University Press, 1999).

M. McDonald, *Ancient Sun, Modern Light. Greek Drama on the Modern Stage* (New York: Columbia University Press 1992).

D. MacDowell, '*Hybris* in Athens', *Greece and Rome* 23 (1976), pp. 14-31.

F. Macintosh, 'Tragedy in Performance: Nineteenth- and Twentieth-century Productions', in Easterling, *Cambridge Companion*, pp. 211-27.

J. March, 'Sophocles' *Ajax*: the Death and Burial of a Hero', *Bulletin of the Institute of Classical Studies* 38 (1991-3), pp. 1-36.

R. Martin, *The Language of Heroes: Speech and Performance in the Iliad* (Ithaca, NY: Cornell University Press, 1989).

C. Martindale, *Redeeming the Text* (Cambridge: Cambridge University Press, 1993).

C. Meier, *The Political Art of Greek Tragedy* (Cambridge: Cambridge University Press, 1993).

S. Mills, *Euripides: Hippolytus* (London: Duckworth, 2002).

J. Moore, 'The dissembling speech of Ajax', *Yale Classical Studies* 25 (1977), pp. 47-66.

J. Montmarquet, 'Epistemic Virtue', in J. Dancy and E. Sosa (editors), *Companion to Epistemology* (Oxford: Basil Blackwell, 1992), pp. 116-18.

I. Morris and B. Powell (editors), *A New Companion to Homer* (Leiden and New York: E.J. Brill, 1997).

G. Most, *The Measures of Praise: Structure and Function in Pindar's Second Pythian and Seventh Nemean Odes* (Göttingen: Vandenhoeck & Ruprecht, 1985).

F. Nisetich, *Pindar and Homer* (Baltimore: Johns Hopkins University Press, 1989).

M. Nussbaum, *The Fragility of Goodness: Luck and Ethics in Greek Tragedy and Philosophy* (Cambridge: Cambridge University Press, 1986).

J. Ober and B. Strauss, 'Drama, Political Rhetoric, and the Discourse of Athenian Democracy', in Winkler and Zeitlin, *Nothing to do with Dionysus?*, pp. 237-70.

Bibliography

D. Ogden, *Greek Bastardy in the Classical and Hellenistic Periods* (Oxford: Clarendon Press, 1996).

K. Ormand, 'Silent by Convention? Sophokles' Tekmessa', *American Journal of Philology* 117 (1996), pp. 37-64.

——— *Exchange and the Maiden: Marriage in Sophoclean Tragedy* (Austin: University of Texas Press, 1999).

E. OKell, 'Does Themistocles' "hero of Salamis" lie behind Sophocles' *Ajax*?', paper delivered to the Joint Classical Association and Classical Association of Scotland Conference, 2002.

R. Osborne and S. Hornblower (editors), *Ritual, Finance, Politics: Democratic Accounts Presented to to David Lewis* (Oxford: Clarendon Press, 1994).

H. Parke, *Festivals of the Athenians* (London: Thames and Hudson, 1977).

R. Parker, *Miasma* (Oxford: Clarendon Press, 1983).

W. Parks, *Verbal Duelling in Heroic Narrative* (Princeton: Princeton University Press, 1990).

Z. Pavlovskis, 'The Voice of the Actor in Greek Tragedy', *Classical World* 71 (1977), pp. 113-23.

C. Pelling (editor), *Characterization and Individuality in Greek Literature* (Oxford: Oxford University Press, 1990).

A. Pickard-Cambridge, *The Dramatic Festivals of Athens*, 2nd ed. revised by J. Gould and D.M. Lewis (Oxford: Clarendon Press, 1988).

L. Pratt, *Lying and Poetry from Homer to Pindar* (Ann Arbor, University of Michigan Press, 1993).

P. Pucci, 'Gods' Intervention and Epiphany', *American Journal of Philology* 115 (1994), pp. 15-46.

W. Race, *Pindar II: Nemean Odes, Isthmian Odes, Fragments*, Loeb Classical Library (Cambridge MA: Harvard University Press, 1997).

H. Rankin, *Antisthenes Sokratikos* (Amsterdam: Hakkert, 1986).

M. Reeve, 'Interpolation in Greek Tragedy III', *Greek, Roman and Byzantine Studies* 14 (1973), pp. 145-71.

R. Rehm, *Greek Tragic Theatre* (London: Routledge, 1992).

K. Reinhardt, *Sophocles* (Oxford: Oxford University Press, 1979).

L. Reynolds and N. Wilson, *Scribes and Scholars*, 3rd ed. (Oxford: Oxford University Press, 1991).

F. Robert, 'Sophocle, Périclès, Hérodote et la date d'*Ajax*', *Revue de Philologie* 38 (1964), pp. 213-27.

P. Rose, 'Historicizing Sophocles' *Ajax*', in Goff, *History, Tragedy, Theory*, pp. 59-90.

D. Rosenbloom, 'Myth, History and Hegemeony in Aeschylus', in Goff, *History, Tragedy, Theory*, pp. 91-130.

——— 'Ajax is *Megas*: is that all we can say?', *Prudentia* 33.2 (2001), pp. 109-30.

——— 'From *Ponêros* to *Pharmakos*: Theater, Social Drama, and

Revolution in Athens, 428-404 BCE', *Classical Antiquity* 21.2 (2002), pp. 283-346.

T. Rosenmeyer, *The Masks of Tragedy: Essays on Six Greek Dramas* (New York: Gordian Press, 1971).

K. Schefold, 'Sophokles' Aias auf einer Lekythos', *Antike Kunst* 19 (1976), pp. 71-8.

G. Schiff, *Johann Heinrich Fuseli 1741-1825*, 2 vols (Zürich: Berichthaus; München: Prestel-Verlas, 1973).

S. Scullion, *Three Studies in Athenian Dramaturgy* (Stuttgart and Leipzig: Teubner, 1994).

R. Seaford, 'Immortality, Salvation and the Elements', *Harvard Studies in Classical Philology* 90 (1986), pp. 1-26.

—— *Reciprocity and Ritual: Homer and Tragedy in the Developing City-State* (Oxford: Oxford University Press, 1994).

—— 'Something to do with Dionysus – Tragedy and the Dionysiac. Response to Friedrich', in Silk, *Tragedy and the Tragic*, pp. 284-94.

—— 'The Social Function of Attic Tragedy: a Response to Jasper Griffin', *Classical Quarterly* 50 (2000), pp. 30-44.

D. Seale, *Vision and Stagecraft in Sophocles* (London: Croom Helm, 1982).

C. Segal, *Dionysiac Poetics and Euripides' Bacchae* (Princeton: Princeton University Press, 1982).

—— 'Sophocles' Praise of Man and the Conflicts of the *Antigone*', *Arion* 3 (1964), pp. 46-66.

—— *Tragedy and Civilization: an Interpretation of Sophocles* (Cambridge MA: Harvard University Press, 1981).

—— *Sophocles' Tragic World: Divinity, Nature, Society* (Cambridge MA, Harvard University Press, 1995).

P. Sellars, 'Peter Sellars' Talk at Carnuntum', in McDonald, *Ancient Sun*, pp. 94-100.

M. Sicherl, 'The Tragic Issue in Sophocles' *Ajax*', *Yale Classical Studies* 25 (1977), pp. 67-98.

P. Siewert, 'The Ephebic Oath in Fifth-Century Athens', *Journal of Hellenic Studies* 97 (1977), pp. 102-11.

M. Silk (editor), *Tragedy and the Tragic: The Greek Theatre and Beyond* (Oxford: Clarendon Press, 1996).

A. Sommerstein, *Aeschylus: the Eumenides* (Cambridge: Cambridge University Press, 1989).

C. Sorum, 'Sophocles' *Ajax* in Context', *Classical World* 79 (1985-6), pp. 361-77.

C. Sourvinou-Inwood, 'Something to do with Athens: Tragedy and Ritual', in Osborne and Hornblower, *Ritual, Finance, Politics*, pp. 269-89.

W. Stanford, 'Light and Darkness Imagery in Sophocles' *Ajax*', *Greek, Roman and Byzantine Studies* 19 (1978), pp. 189-97.

——— *Sophocles Ajax* (London: Macmillan, 1963; revised edition Bristol: Bristol Classical Press, 1981).

B. Strauss, *Fathers and Sons in Athens* (Princeton: Princeton University Press, 1993).

K. Synodinou, 'Tecmessa in the *Ajax* of Sophocles', *Antike und Abendland* 33 (1987), pp. 99-107.

R. Talbert, *Plutarch on Sparta* (Harmondsworth: Penguin, 1988).

O. Taplin, *The Stagecraft of Aeschylus* (Oxford: Clarendon Press, 1977).

——— *Greek Tragedy in Action* (London: Methuen, 1978).

——— 'Yielding to Forethought: Sophocles' *Ajax*', in G. Bowersock, W. Burkert and M. Putnam (editors), *Arktouros: Hellenic Studies Presented to B.M.W. Knox* (Berlin: de Gruyter, 1979), pp. 122-9.

——— 'Comedy and the Tragic', in Silk, *Tragedy and the Tragic*, pp. 188-202.

R. Torrance, 'Sophocles: some Bearings', *Harvard Studies in Classical Philology* 69 (1965), pp. 269-327.

P. Vidal-Naquet, *The Black Hunter: Forms of Thought and Forms of Society in the Greek World* (Baltimore and London: Johns Hopkins University Press, 1986).

——— *Fragments sur l'Art Antique* (Paris: Agnès Viénot Éditions, 2002).

G. Vlastos, 'Equality and Justice in Early Greek Cosmologies', *Classical Philology* 42 (1947), pp. 156-78.

G. Walsh, *The Varieties of Enchantment* (Chapel Hill: University of North Carolina Press, 1984).

T. Webster, *Greek Theatre Production* (London: Methuen, 1956).

——— *An Introduction to Sophocles*, 2nd ed. (London: Methuen, 1969).

C. Whitman, *Sophocles: a Study of Heroic Humanism* (Cambridge MA: Harvard University Press, 1951).

——— *Homer and the Heroic Tradition* (Cambridge MA: Harvard University Press, 1958).

M. Wigodsky, 'The "Salvation" of Ajax', *Hermes* 90 (1962), pp. 149-58.

J. Wilders (editor), *Samuel Butler: Hudibras* (Oxford: Clarendon Press, 1967).

D. Wiles, *Tragedy in Athens* (Cambridge: Cambridge University Press, 1997).

B. Williams, *Shame and Necessity* (Berkeley, University of California Press, 1993).

P. Wilson, 'Demosthenes 21 (*Against Meidias*): Democratic Abuse', *Proceedings of the Cambridge Philological Society* 37 (1991), 164-95.

——— *The Athenian Institution of the Khorêgia: the Chorus, the City and the Stage* (Cambridge: Cambridge University Press, 2000).

J. Winkler and F. Zeitlin (editors), *Nothing to do with Dionysus?* (Princeton: Princeton University Press, 1990).

Bibliography

R. Winnington-Ingram, *Sophocles: an Interpretation* (Cambridge: Cambridge University Press, 1980).

V. Wohl, *Intimate Commerce: Exchange, Gender and Subjectivity in Greek Tragedy* (Austin: University of Texas Press, 1998).

N. Worman, 'Odysseus *Panourgos*. The Liar's Style in Tragedy and Oratory', *Helios* 26.1 (1999), pp. 35-68.

—————— 'The *Herkos Achaiôn* Transformed: Character Type and Spatial Meaning in the *Ajax*', *Classical Philology* 96 (2001), pp. 228-52.

G. Zanker, 'Sophocles' *Ajax* and the Heroic Values of the *Iliad*', *Classical Quarterly* 42 (1992), pp. 20-5.

Glossary

Agôn. 'Contest' or 'debate scene' consisting of a monologue by one character on an issue central to the tragedy, answered by a second speech attempting a refutation of the first speaker's position. A dialogue (often including *stichomythia*) between the two speakers follows.

Aidôs, aidoumai. Noun and verb covering 'shame', 'self-restraint' and 'reverence'. Ajax is ashamed of his failure and humiliation while Tecmessa uses these terms to stress the shamefulness of abandoning his *philoi* through suicide.

Aretê. 'Excellence' or 'virtue'.

Charis. Gratitude, favour, positive reciprocity.

Ekkuklêma. Wheeled wooden platform, located inside the *skênê* building and rolled out of it when the playwright shows a scene taking place indoors or the results of 'indoors' action. In our play, Ajax's second entrance may be on the platform even though this is not technically an 'indoors' scene.

Episode. Scene of a tragedy often (but not always) divided by a *stasimon* or a *parodos*.

Êthos. 'Character', but see p. 133 for the difficulty of this translation.

Eugeneia. Good birth or 'nobility'.

Exodos. Final scene of a tragedy.

Hubris. Insolence, outrage, physical violence. On the question of how far it implies an impious and arrogant action or attitude towards the gods, see pp. 146-8.

Intertextuality, intertext. To put it simply, intertextuality describes the process when a text's meaning is partly generated through its invocation of, or interaction with, the language, characters and even specific episodes or phrases of another text or genre of texts. An 'intertext' is any text which has an intertextual relationship with the text under prime consideration. Thus *Iliad* 6 is an intertext for *Ajax*.

Kleos. Glory, fame in song.

Megas. This word, and other forms beginning *meg-*, mean 'big' or 'great'. The opposite is *smikros* and other words with the root *mikr*, meaning 'small'. In our play it is a key epithet for Ajax but the issue of who is 'big' and what 'bigness' consists of is contested in the post-death scenes.

Nomos, nomoi. 'Custom', 'customs'. Also used of laws, codes and conventions. In opposition to *phusis* it implies culture and civic order.

Ômos. 'Savage', 'raw', 'wild'.

Orchêstra. 'Dancing place'. Part of the stage where the chorus performed, but we do not know that they were *confined* to this space and actors probably used it too.

Parodos. Song sung by the chorus on their first entry.

Phronimos. 'Sane'.

Phusis. Nature

Prologue. Opening scene of the play (prior to the *parodos*).

Philia. 'Friendship' or 'kinship'.

Philos, philoi (fem. philê, philai). 'Friend', 'friends', or 'relative', 'relatives' (in the sense of 'kin').

Skênê. Building on the stage which stood for any place entered by characters in a tragedy. Can also mean 'tent' or 'hut' and our play may exploit this ambiguity.

Sôphrosunê. 'Safe-mindedness'. But it also implies 'self-control', 'good sense', 'virtue' or 'moderation' depending on the context of utterance and the agenda of the speaker. In our play, it is often implicitly glossed as 'obedience to a higher authority'. There is often a contrast between *sôphrosunê* and *hubris* in Athenian texts.

Stasimon. Song sung by the chorus (also known as a choral ode) which often divides episodes.

Stichomythia. A kind of stylised conversation between actors who speak to one another in alternating lines. Its dramatic and thematic effects and connotations vary, but in our play it is used when one character is eliciting information from another, when excitement through speedy dialogue is needed, when characters are arguing or verbal duelling. Antagonistic stichomythia rarely ends in resolution.

Timê. Honour.

Xenia. Guest-friendship. This is often the result of alliances forged between families or a bond brought about by the offering and receipt of hospitality or (as in the case of Hector and Ajax) a strange business of forming a bond with your enemy via a gift-exchange after combat.

Chronology

Some adaptations and other forms of 'reception' listed here are not discussed in the text. Further details of sources, editions and illustrations for extant post-classical items can be found in J. Davidson Reid, *The Oxford Guide to Classical Mythology and the Arts 1300-1990*, vol. 1 (Oxford: Oxford University Press, 1993), pp. 78-80. This list of productions, translations and adaptations is indicative rather than exhaustive.

BC
c. **750-800**: Probable date of Homer's *Iliad* and *Odyssey*.
700-600: Judgement of Arms often represented on Greek Vases (e.g. *LIMC* 1.1 325.72). Earliest depiction of Ajax's suicide on proto-Corinthian vase (*LIMC* 1.1 330.118).
c. **534/3**: Tradition that Thespis' tragedy wins at City Dionysia.
508/7: Cleisthenes' reforms. Beginning of democracy at Athens.
501: City Dionysia reorganised; official contest records begin.
c. **496/5**: Birth of Sophocles.
490-479: Persian Wars.
484: Aeschylus' first victory in dramatic contest.
472: Aeschylus' *Persians*.
468: Sophocles' first victory in dramatic contest (with *Triptolemus*).
462: Reforms of Ephialtes; extension of democracy at Athens.
461-446: First so-called 'Peloponnesian war' between Athens and Corinth (and occasionally Sparta).
455: Euripides competes for first time (comes third).
451/0: Pericles' citizenship law.
450-440?: Decade which most critics think likely for performance of *Ajax*.
449: Competition for best tragic actor begun at City Dionysia.
431-404: Second 'Peloponnesian war' between Athens and Sparta.
406/5: Death of Sophocles.
c. **400-350**: Antisthenes' speeches, *Ajax* and *Odysseus*.
c. **375**: *Ajax*, tragedy by Carcinus.
c. **360**: *Ajax Mad*, tragedy by Astydamas.

c. 330: *Ajax*, tragedy by Theodectes.

c. 240-169: Roman poets Livius Andronicus and Ennius produce Latin adaptations of *Ajax*.

220-130: Roman playwright Pacuvius adapts Sophocles' *Teucer* and *Judgement of Arms*.

170-c. 86: Roman playwright and scholar Accius writes a *Judgement*. His *Eurysaces* is performed in the mid-first century BC.

AD

c. 4-8: Ovid *Metamorphoses* Book 13 (hexameter poem).

c. 150-200?: Lucian *Dialogues of the Dead* 23, 'Ajax and Agamemnon'. Hyginus compiles a handbook of mythology based on Greek sources and Ajax is in it (*Fabulae* 107, 116).

c. 1316-28: Contest of Ajax and Ulysses and death of Ajax in *Ovid Moralisé* (anonymous French allegorised elaboration of Ovid's *Metamorphoses*).

1538-9: 'The Death of Ajax', fresco after designs by Italian painter Giulio Romana in the Sala di Troia, Palazzo Ducale, Mantua.

1579: 'Ajax runs on his sword', fresco by Italian painter Giovanni Battista Castello in Giovanelli Castle, Gorlago.

1582: *Tragedia de Ayax Telemón*, tragedy, after Sophocles, by Spanish writer Juan de la Cueva.

1596: *A New Discourse of a Stale Subject Called the Metamorphosis of Ajax*, satirical treatise by Sir John Harington.

1608: Translation of Sophocles' *Ajax* by German writer Wolfhart Spangenberg.

1614: *Ayax and Ulisses*, tragedy by Dutch writer Pieter Hooft.

c. 1645-58: *The Contention of Ajax and Ulysses for the Armor of Achilles*, an 'entertainment' by James Shirley, possibly performed at his grammar school in London.

1684: *Ajax*, tragedy by Jean de La Chapelle perfomed in Paris.

1694-7: *L'Aiace*, opera first performed in the Taetro Ducale, Milan. Libretto by P. d'Averara. This Libretto used in several different Italian productions.

c. 1698: 'The suicide of Ajax', Spanish School painting.

1700: *The Speeches of Ajax and Ulysses*, poem by John Dryden; translation of Ovid *Metamorphoses* 13.

1714: *Ajax*, tragedy after Sophocles by Nicholas Rowe performed in London. Another version in the same year by Lewis Theobald.

1758-60: *La Mort d'Ajax*, ballet choreographed by Jean-Georges Noverre and first performed in Lyons.

1768-1812: Series of paintings and drawings depicting Ajax's tragedy and afterlife by Henry Fuseli.

1789: *Ajax und Tekmessa*, drama by August K. Borheck.

c. 1803: Fragment of translation of *Ajax* by Friedrich Hölderlin.

201

1873: *Ajas*, tragedy in verse by Otto Franz Gensichen.

1882: *Ajax* performed in Greek at the first Cambridge Greek play.

1893: Floris Stempel and his friends found the now world-class Amsterdam football club *Ajax FC*. They changed the name to this because it was 'more chic' than their previous name 'Union'. At this time, just as Greek tragedy and antiquity were in vogue, it was fashionable in England and Holland to name new clubs and leagues after figures or places from ancient Greek mythology and history (e.g. *Sparta Rotterdam*, *Achilles Hengelo*, and *Corinthians*). *Ajax FC's* logo still depicts the head of the hero.

1904: *Ajax* performed by local Greek community in Clinton Community Hall, New York. Directed by Mabel Hay Barrows.

1905: *Ajax*, a novel by Johanna Niemann.

1907: One scene of an unfinished *Ajax*, drama by André Gide.

1940: *Ajax*, orchestral suite by Riccardo Zandonai.

1949-54: 'Ajax', painting by Georges Braque.

1961: *Ajax*, production by the Greek National Theatre.

1971: *Die Ermordung des Aias* ('The suicide of Ajax'), drama by Hartmut Lange.

1972: *Ajax*, first performance of composition for baritone and orchestra by John Eaton. Text after Sophocles.

1986: *Ajax*, version of Sophocles' tragedy written by R. Auletta. Production directed by P. Sellars and performed in California and Washington DC.

Oliver Stone's film, *Platoon*.

Index

Achilles 32-3, 35, 39, 40-1, 59,
61-3, 64, 99, 140, 167
actors 13, 101-3, 114, 163, 177
Aeschylus 12, 18, 19-20, 112,
131, 147-8
Aethiopis 26
Agamemnon: ancestry attacked
121-2; attack on Teucer 120-3;
attitude to Ajax 120-30;
exchange with Odysseus 126-
30; in *Ajax* 107, 120-30; in
epic 26; *see also* Atreids
agôn, *see* debate scenes
Aiantis tribe 21-4
aidôs, *see* shame
Ajax *passim*; and Achilles 32-3,
40-1, 59, 60-3; and Athena 40-
7, 96-7, 110, 122; and claims
to the arms, 36-9; and
Eurysaces 69-73, 135; and
deception speech 74-95; and
harshness 77, 114; and intellect 93-7; and Odysseus, 40-7,
58-9, 61-2, 124-5; and pity 77-
8, 92; and polis 21, 35, 111,
113, 124; and suicide 97-103,
120; and Tecmessa, 55-7, 63-
73, 74-5, 92, 135; and
Telamon 60-3, 108-9; and
Teucer 105-30; as 'bulwark'
50, 119, 166; as 'tower' 25, 28-
9, 35; boastfulness and
arrogance of 59, 96-7, 114,
130; choice of lives, 62-3, 108-
9; corpse of 101-3, 106-7, 110,
178; doubleness of 120; duel

with Hector 33-4, 123-4;
extremism of 21, 33, 59, 96-7,
99-103, 125, 134-41; his failures of reciprocity 49, 67,
74-5, 90, 122; his humiliation
58, 60-3, 109, 143-4; in epic
cycle 26; in hero-cult 20-4; in
Homer 24-7, 32-4; in Pindar
36-9; in texts and art after
Sophocles 148-62; in vase
painting 154, 163, 164;
madness of 54-7, 73, 136-41;
sarcastic tone 81, 83, 85;
savagery of 70-1, 120; sense of
pride 84; severity of 69-71, 73,
92; supplication of 118-20;
vulnerability of 29-30; *see also*
character; deception speech;
hero-cult; heroism; *hubris*;
philia; reciprocity
Alcaeus 34-6, 167
alternation 48, 77, 82-3, 90, 116
ambiguity 41, 75, 85, 92-5
Anaximander 82, 89
Andromache 67-70
Antisthenes 150-2, 182
Aristotle: on 'possible worlds' 19;
on *charis* (reciprocity) 65-6;
on friendship 85; on 'intellectual virtue' 93-4; on Sophocles
14; on the polis 54; on tragic
character 132-4
Astyanax 67
Athena 40-7, 63, 79, 96-7, 112,
139, 141, 143-8, 155
Athenian democracy 31, 49-50,

203

CPSIA information can be obtained
at www.ICGtesting.com
Printed in the USA
LVOW03s1910250717
542598LV00015B/266/P